Praise for *Dec...*

"Doreen Virtue not only provides a fascinating account of how the Lord led her from error to truth and from darkness to light, but she also provides wise and needed cautions about how the kind of faulty thinking that she earlier championed has infiltrated the church. Those who read it will thus benefit not just from an exciting and encouraging conversion story, but also by way of the enhanced discernment needed in an age of widespread biblical illiteracy."

—RANDAL ROBERTS, DMIN, PRESIDENT AND
PROFESSOR OF CHRISTIAN SPIRITUALITY,
WESTERN SEMINARY, PORTLAND, OREGON

"Doreen Virtue is a wonderful example of a life made new in Jesus Christ, and her story is important for the world to hear. She has an experience and a perspective most Christians don't have, having been an influential voice in the New Age movement. What Jesus led her into—a deep and true knowledge of God in and through God's Word—is an even better story."

—DAVID GUZIK, AUTHOR AND BIBLE COMMENTATOR

"Writing from the heart but using God's Word as sure footing, Doreen Virtue recounts her experiences in Christian Science and the New Age and how she unexpectedly came into the light of Christ, an event that turned her life upside down but also gave her the peace she had sought but never found. This book will be helpful and encouraging to Christians as well as revealing to those who might be dabbling in the New Age."

—MARCIA MONTENEGRO, FOUNDER, CHRISTIAN ANSWERS
FOR THE NEW AGE; AUTHOR OF *SPELLBOUND: THE
PARANORMAL SEDUCTION OF TODAY'S KIDS*

"There is nothing new about the New Age movement. It's in reality an old age movement that began when Adam sinned, and then tried to hide from God. This publication pulls back the fig leaves with love, with gentleness, with brutal honesty, and with sound biblical doctrine. May God use this fascinating and wonderfully insightful book to bring many to the truth that is alone in Jesus."

—RAY COMFORT, CEO AND FOUNDER OF LIVINGWATERS.COM

"Beautifully written book that documents Doreen's experiences in the New Age, and her painful account of facing persecution while being in the public eye after renouncing her New Age involvement to follow Jesus Christ. Doreen holds nothing back, and fearlessly exposes deception, while shining a light on biblical truth. As a former New Ager myself, I found myself reliving many of her same experiences. Excellent book, and highly recommended source to bring those out of deception."

—TARA CHELIOUDAKIS, AUTHOR OF *THE NARROW PATH: ESCAPING THE GRIPS OF DECEPTION WHILE DISCOVERING HIS WAY, LIFE, AND TRUTH*

"Rarely do we get a glimpse into the life and thinking of a former false prophet. Doreen expresses genuine sorrow and lovingly points the reader to the Scriptures in her revealing, personal journey out of deception. I pray that those within the New Age, and those within Christ's church will recognize the demonic spiritual realities behind experiences and practices not grounded in Scripture."

—BRANDON KIMBER, FILMMAKER, DIRECTOR OF *AMERICAN GOSPEL: CHRIST ALONE*

"*Deceived No More* exposes deceptive New Age doctrine and practices through Doreen's captivating, yet informative, story. Those directly affected by New Age teachings will find it life-giving. Those who aren't will be surprised to learn just how much these teachings have influenced the culture, and even the church. But, enlightening as it may be, *Deceived No More* is, above all, a beautiful testament to the mercy and saving grace of Christ."

—MICHELLE LESLEY, WOMEN'S DISCIPLESHIP BLOGGER AND SPEAKER, MICHELLELESLEY.COM

"Read this book to save yourself or others from years of regret and deception. *Deceived No More* is filled with insider insights into the New Age movement and gems of spiritual discernment. Doreen shares advice gleaned from her own painful lessons, after realizing she had spent most of her life as a false prophet leading others into falsehood. This book sounds the alarm in a culture where New Age teachings have been mainstreamed and are even gaining entrance into Christian churches through a growing movement of self-declared 'apostles' and 'prophets.'"

—HOLLY PIVEC, COAUTHOR OF *GOD'S SUPER-APOSTLES:
ENCOUNTERING THE WORLDWIDE PROPHETS AND APOSTLES
MOVEMENT*; FOUNDER OF SPIRITOFERROR.ORG

"This book has something for just about everyone, including atheists, the rich and famous, new believers, New Agers, those involved with mysticism, the religious, as well as seasoned Christians. We could all glean a lot from this book, especially when it comes to discerning truth from error. Not only has Doreen's salvation and testimony already blessed numerous people, her new efforts continue to impact many all over the world. I am looking forward to see how her book will continue to fulfill her longing to help individuals all over the globe."

—MARK BAKER, AUTHOR OF *DIVINE DESIGN, GOD'S BLUEPRINT
FOR A THRIVING MARRIAGE*; FOUNDER AND DIRECTOR OF
HOPE FOR LIFE BIBLICAL COUNSELING AND EQUIPPING
MINISTRY, WWW.HOPEFORLIFEONLINE.COM/

"Doreen Virtue has the most significant public testimony in the history of alternative spirituality. Her story is an incredible display of God's saving grace, and her journey through the occult to Christ as outlined in this book is so mind-blowing that anything short of a miracle can't explain it. This is an absolute must-read."

—STEVEN BANCARZ, FORMER NEW AGE TEACHER, BESTSELLING
AUTHOR OF *THE SECOND COMING OF THE NEW AGE*

Deceived No More

Deceived
No More

How Jesus Led Me out of the
New Age and into His Word

DOREEN
VIRTUE

EMANATE
BOOKS

Published in Nashville, Tennessee, by Emanate Books, an imprint of Thomas Nelson. Emanate Books and Thomas Nelson are registered trademarks of HarperCollins Christian Publishing, Inc.

Thomas Nelson titles may be purchased in bulk for educational, business, fund-raising, or sales promotional use. For information, please e-mail SpecialMarkets@ThomasNelson.com.

Unless otherwise noted, Scripture quotations are taken from the ESV® Bible (The Holy Bible, English Standard Version®). Copyright © 2001 by Crossway, a publishing ministry of Good News Publishers. Used by permission. All rights reserved.

Scripture quotations marked KJV are from the King James Version. Public domain.

Scripture quotations marked NASB are from New American Standard Bible®. Copyright © 1960, 1962, 1963, 1968, 1971, 1972, 1973, 1975, 1977, 1995 by The Lockman Foundation. Used by permission. (www.Lockman.org)

Scripture quotations marked NIV are from the Holy Bible, New International Version®, NIV®. Copyright © 1973, 1978, 1984, 2011 by Biblica, Inc.® Used by permission of Zondervan. All rights reserved worldwide. www.Zondervan.com. The "NIV" and "New International Version" are trademarks registered in the United States Patent and Trademark Office by Biblica, Inc.®

Scripture quotations marked NKJV are from the New King James Version®. © 1982 by Thomas Nelson. Used by permission. All rights reserved.

Scripture quotations marked NLT are from the Holy Bible, New Living Translation. © 1996, 2004, 2007, 2013, 2015 by Tyndale House Foundation. Used by permission of Tyndale House Publishers, Inc., Carol Stream, Illinois 60188. All rights reserved.

Any Internet addresses, phone numbers, or company or product information printed in this book are offered as a resource and are not intended in any way to be or to imply an endorsement by Thomas Nelson, nor does Thomas Nelson vouch for the existence, content, or services of these sites, phone numbers, companies, or products beyond the life of this book.

ISBN 978-0-7852-3422-7 (eBook)
ISBN 978-0-7852-3410-4 (TP)

Library of Congress Control Number: 2020936490

20 21 22 23 24   LSC   10 9 8 7 6 5 4 3 2 1

Contents

CONTENTS

Introduction

Confessions of a Former False Prophet

It's a miracle that I'm writing this book, and a testimony to God's sovereignty. I pray that this book will give you insight into the mind of a New Age false prophet so that you can detect and avoid deception yourself.

The Bible warns us of the dangers of following a false prophet. False prophets can lead us away from salvation, as I discovered in following the false prophet Mary Baker Eddy since childhood. If I'd died before learning about and having faith in the true Jesus and the true gospel, I could've been cast into eternal torment. So, this topic is a salvific issue. Unsaved people who follow false teachers may never hear the gospel. They may never learn who Jesus truly is and why He had to die for us. To be saved from eternal damnation that we all earn for our sins (Romans 3:23; 6:23), we must confess that Jesus is Lord and believe in our hearts that God raised Jesus from the dead (Romans 10:9–11).

I also pray that if you have loved ones who are following false prophets, this book will help you understand their mindset, which is useful for your witnessing.

In addition, I've written this book to support those who've come out of deception, and who have post-traumatic symptoms and re-occurring thoughts about the past. May the pages of this book offer you comfort and practical solutions, as well as encouragement that Jesus can turn around anyone's life.

On January 7, 2017, I had a profound experience that catapulted me out of my career as a top-selling New Age author: I surrendered my life to Jesus as my Lord and Savior. I lost almost everything and everyone in order to follow Jesus, as you'll read in this book. I went from a first-class lifestyle to becoming a humble servant starting over at age fifty-eight and entering seminary at age sixty. I endured cruel slander, gossip, and persecution from New Agers who took my conversion as a personal betrayal and who insisted that I somehow instantly get my old products off the market (even though I wasn't selling the items myself and had asked my former publishers to stop selling them).

This is my story of learning to trust God after nearly wasting a lifetime being independent and willful. I stopped trying to predict and control the future and instead learned to lean on God's sovereignty. Jesus saved my soul from deception and opened my eyes to His truth. I'm grieved over what I experienced and did during my time as a New Age teacher. I'm a wretched sinner, as you'll read in these pages. My life was a train wreck because I previously followed New Age principles. Before Jesus saved me, I was heading straight to hell without realizing it.

This book purposely avoids some of the topics that I see Christians bickering about. So you won't find discussions about Calvinism versus Arminianism in these pages. As Charles Spurgeon said, "Satan does not care whether he drags you down to hell as a Calvinist or as an Arminian, so long as he can get you there."[1]

The book also doesn't contain theories or interpretations about eschatology. I watch Christians debate about pre-mil versus post-mil, and I think, *Only God knows what will happen. Our role is to prepare for Jesus' return, not to quarrel about its timeline.* The purpose of this book is to inform people about the underbelly and nuances of the New Age, to help you notice and avoid its deception that has been creeping into the church. So, this book focuses on primary issues that could potentially affect salvation.

Writing this testimony book and remembering my past have been stomach churning and soul searing. I also went through considerable spiritual warfare while writing these pages, mostly in the form of the enemy trying to distract me away from writing. Thank you to the Holy Spirit for helping me focus!

During my years of darkness, I wasn't a rebellious Christian but a biblically ignorant and foolish unsaved person who didn't know the true gospel because I didn't understand sin and hadn't studied the Bible. Recalling my past beliefs while writing this book has been an emotional experience for me. As a relatively new person in Christ, I barely recognize my pre-salvation self.

It's also painful for me to write about the false gospel of Christian Science that I grew up in, because my mother still adheres to its principles and attends its meetings as I write this. She becomes angry and defensive when she hears me discuss Christian Science deception. My born-again brother, Ken, and I have shared the true gospel and the issues with Christian Science, yet she still defends Mary Baker Eddy. I love my mother dearly and pray that she'll be saved and repent from false teachings and turn to the true gospel of Jesus Christ. I welcome your prayers for her salvation as well.

No amount of slander or gossip about me can adequately describe the sin I committed while I was blinded by deception, as you'll read in this confessional book. I was unknowingly teaching heresy as a false prophet in the New Age because I hadn't taken the time to study Scripture. Through my previous work, some people were led away from Jesus and the Bible, which endlessly grieves me today. That's why I say that my salvation is a miracle, because I certainly didn't deserve or earn it. God opened my eyes and saved me by His unmerited grace and mercy.

I've repented and know that God has graciously and mercifully forgiven me. Even though I'm forgiven, I'm dealing with the painful consequences of my sin, and I pray that others will learn from my mistakes and also learn how to avoid deception. All those years, I didn't know that I was following a false Christ and heretical doctrine. I honestly didn't know that I was rebelling against God. I was so spiritually blind that I actually believed I was helping God save the world through my New Age teachings.

Had I read Jesus' warnings in the Gospels earlier in my life, or read a Christian discernment book like this one, I might've been able to avoid years of pain and suffering. So I'm grateful that you're reading this book right now.

I also trust that our sovereign God is using my past for His glory. As Romans 8:28 promises, "For those who love God all things work together for good, for those who are called according to his purpose."

You see, I was born and raised in a false religion (Christian Science), which led me into the New Age. Christian Science was invented by the false prophet Mary Baker Eddy and her teacher, Phineas Quimby. Eddy heretically declared that she'd received personal revelation of the Bible's true meaning; then she proceeded to shred the gospel. Christian Science belongs to a movement called "New Thought." The Religious Science and Unity Church organizations also belong to the movement. New Thought is a cousin to New Age teachings, with common roots and beliefs. It's also related to the "prosperity gospel," as I'll discuss in this book.

In adulthood, I became the top-selling New Age author at the top-selling New Age publishing house. I realize now that in many ways, I was teaching the Christian Science false gospel in my books and seminars. I gave sold-out workshops around the world and appeared on countless television programs, including *Oprah*, *The View*, CNN, *Richard and Judy* (UK), and more. Celebrities freely promoted my products. I don't say all of that to boast, but to give glory to God for

His miracle in saving me out of extreme depths of deception. I was so blind back then that I didn't realize I was sinning and needed a savior.

Because people constantly told me that my New Age work was comforting and helpful, and because I hadn't read the whole Bible, I didn't realize that I was teaching a heretical doctrine and leading others to a false Christ. I thought I was helping people, so, therefore, I must be pleasing God, right? Well, that was the lesson I needed to learn: there's a big difference between comforting and truly helping a person. My old work was "comforting people in their sins" and making them feel comfortable in continuing to practice pagan actions and beliefs. Leading people to Jesus and the Bible would have been truly helpful, and I was doing the opposite.

In my upside-down New Age way of thinking, I believed I was doing God's work. I often referred to myself as "God's secretary" and said that I was an "open-minded Christian." This is where I now cringe, do a face-palm, and repent because I was deceived by a false light that was actually darkness. Tragically and unknowingly, I passed that deception along to others, including my children. This is my story to help warn others about deception and to share how Jesus saved me. This is vital information, because the enemy is an evil genius who can craftily enter your life and your church, disguised as an angel of light, a servant of righteousness, a workman, or an apostle (2 Corinthians 11:13–15).

In my family's false religion of Christian Science (which is neither Christian nor scientific), I was taught a heresy that I can barely speak of now: the belief that Jesus was just a man who demonstrated a potential that we all could attain. This is called the heresy of "Arianism," where Jesus is viewed as a created human instead of as He truly is: the second person of our Holy Trinity, who was fully God *and* fully human during His earthly ministry. Just like the false religions of Jehovah's Witness and Mormonism, Christian Science was based on one person's "divine revelations" instead of on the Holy Bible.

The whole focus of our religion was to learn how to spiritually heal disease and injuries. It was like the prosperity gospel, except that instead of praying to acquire wealth, we used formulaic prayers to acquire health.

Now, don't get me wrong: I do believe that God does miraculous healing work today. But the Christian Science formula, like the prosperity gospel, puts the focus on our own human power instead of God's power. It teaches that if you have enough faith and can get your mind above the physical plane, then your health will automatically shift back to being in God's image of perfect, whole, and complete. If you didn't heal, it meant that your mind was holding a negative or "mortal mind" belief. You didn't have enough faith. We never once acknowledged that sickness or injury may be God's will, because we hadn't studied the book of Job or the fact that Paul learned to live with a thorn in his side (2 Corinthians 12:7).

Christian Science also emphasizes "experiences" above studying the Bible in its entirety. My mother once told me that the primary purpose of Jesus' earthly ministry was to teach us all how to have good physical health. Christian Scientists and New Agers don't consider their eternity or the health of their souls. They just use "positive affirmations" so they won't think about what they consider to be a "negative" topic.

I was also taught that there was no crucifixion, no devil, no sin, and no hell, and anyone who said otherwise was just being negative. The only "sin" was being unkind, fearful, or negative. The fall described in Genesis 3 was just a metaphorical myth according to the Christian Science teachings I grew up learning.[2]

That's why hearing the gospel didn't convict me, because I was stubbornly certain that I wasn't a sinner. Why would I need a savior if I wasn't a sinner? Why would I need saving? In my upbringing, the concept of "sin" was an illusion. We humans hadn't fallen; we'd just become "negative." So long as I stayed positive, I would be "spiritually safe." Sounds crazy, doesn't it? Yet that's the upside-down doctrine of New Age and New Thought teachings. And that's why New Agers judge Christians as being negative for saying that we're all sinners. Back then, if you called me a *sinner*, it was the same as calling me a cuss word. You were insulting me personally with that word, because according to the doctrine I was raised in, I was God's perfect child who could do whatever I wanted as long as I stayed positive.

In other words, I was taught heresy. But how would I realize that as a child? I believed my mom when she said we were Christians. After all, we read passages from the King James Version Bible, we prayed, we attended church twice weekly, and we used Christian terminology. Later I'd realize that a lot of false teachings use Christian terms while twisting scripture and espousing a false gospel.

You see, we only read bits and pieces of the Bible from the weekly "Christian Science Lesson," which were prescribed verses given to church members. We'd only quote the cherry-picked verses that fit our theology. Even then, we'd twist these verses to support our heretical beliefs. For example, we thought "Be still, and know that I am God" (Psalm 46:10) meant to quietly meditate on the fact that we ourselves were little gods in training to be masters like Jesus. Yet, that verse is actually God's voice saying that *He* is God, and that we should relax and trust Him.

We constantly took verses out of context, like Jesus saying that we could do all these things and more in John 14:12. In the New Age and Christian Science, we thought that meant we could perform even greater miracles than Jesus. Yet, in context we see that this verse means that with our modern age of global transportation and connectivity, we're now able to spread the gospel farther than Jesus and the disciples could in their day.[3]

We New Agers also took the fact that the Bible had the word *meditate* in it as proof that it was okay to indulge in Eastern forms of meditation. Well, there's a big difference between Eastern meditation practices that involve emptying your mind and biblical meditation. Eastern practices are open invitations for demons to put ungodly ideas into your head. Believe me, I know all about that unfortunate outcome, because my most outrageous teachings were the result of "insights" I received during Eastern types of meditation sessions.

Jesus also warned against repetitive prayer, which could include repeatedly reciting a word (such as a mantra or contemplative prayer words) when he said, "And when you pray, do not use vain repetitions as the heathen do. For they think that they will be heard for their many words" (Matthew 6:7 NKJV). The idea behind Eastern forms of meditation and contemplative prayer is to reach inside for secret wisdom, to find God, or to connect with the universe.[4]

It's biblical *and* spiritually safer to practice the form of meditation that the Bible speaks about. The word *meditate* in biblical Hebrew is *hagah*, which means "to meditate, moan, growl, utter, speak," referring to sighing, moaning, musing, or verbally repeating what you're reading out of the Bible. So when the Bible says in Joshua 1:8 and Psalm 1:2 to meditate day and night upon the Law (the first five books of the Bible), it means to utter aloud while reading Scripture.[5]

In the New Age and Christian Science, we used an incorrect method of Bible study called *eisegesis* (pronounced: ice-seh-jee-sis). Eisegesis means that you begin your Bible reading with a self-made premise; then you dig for verses to support your premise. For example, an ambitious person wants to amass great wealth and fame, so he uses Philippians 4:13, "I can do all things through Him who strengthens me" as his proof text that God will help him succeed in the worldly sense. That's an example of eisegesis, where verses are used to support an outside idea instead of interpreted as the author intended.

How do we know the biblical author's intention? By reading the passages before and after the verse. This is called *exegesis* (pronounced: ex-eh-jee-sis). For example, we correctly interpret Philippians 4:13 by reading the circumstances that Paul was writing about, which were that he was learning to withstand the suffering of being imprisoned in a dank Roman cell. He also learned how to deal with those times when his life was improved. No matter how sad, painful, or unhappy his circumstances, Paul leaned on the strength of Jesus to endure. That's exegesis, and you can see that it has nothing to do with acquiring abundance, or even health or a love life (which only eisegesis would find). Philippians 4 is all about how to deal with suffering in godly ways, which is a more valuable lesson than any material gain we could acquire.

The Bible is meant to be read through the lens of exegesis. This means that when you read the Bible, you don't decide ahead of time what those verses mean. Instead, the words through the Holy Spirit inform you of their meaning. Exegesis also involves "hermeneutics" (pronounced: her-meh-new-ticks), the process of comparing what Scripture says elsewhere in the Bible to properly understand and interpret the Scripture we're presently reading. With eisegesis, we incorrectly search for verses to support whatever we want. With exegesis, Scripture does all the teaching and informing, through its author, the Holy Spirit.

The error of eisegesis comes from deciding what you want Scripture to say. Sometimes this involves the imagination, as for Mary Baker Eddy, who decided that she was the appointed person to explain the entire Bible through Christian Science. First, she created a "glossary" of Bible terms to "explain the true meaning" of these terms. For example, she wrote that *evening* really means "mistiness of mortal thought; weariness of mortal mind; obscured views; peace and light."[6] Her glossary has no references to specific Scripture text.

As discernment commentator Dr. James Sire wrote, "Mary Baker Eddy moves easily from plain biblical terms to eccentric, spiritual meanings on, as it appears, no particular basis but her own imagination."[7] That's what she did when she "defined" the Holy Trinity as consisting of Life, Truth, and Love. Doesn't that heresy sound lovely on the surface? Yet, it's neither biblical nor helpful in knowing the true nature of the Father, the Son, and the Holy Spirit. Sire says that unless we are prepared to view Eddy as a special prophet receiving new revelation, there's no reason to use her glossary as a guide.[8]

Mary Baker Eddy was practiced as a spiritualist, clairvoyant, and medium, according to her biographers, who have recorded that she would go into trance states and deliver messages from the biblical apostles, Abraham Lincoln, and Jesus Christ.[9] Obviously, she was not channeling Jesus, the apostles, or Lincoln, but was oppressed by masquerading demons enticing her to create a new religion that would fulfill her dreams of recognition.

Like Mary Baker Eddy, I was a false prophet who taught and wrote whatever entered my mind. As time went on and my popularity grew, I became narcissistic and never questioned the validity of what popped into my head. Anyone who criticized my work was wrong, in my old mindset. I didn't realize until after Jesus saved me that I'd been a false prophet, and it's possible Eddy didn't realize her apostasy either.

By the way, you'll see me use the word *apostasy* (pronounced uh-poss-stuh-see) occasionally, so let's define it. *Apostasy*, from the Greek word *apostasia*, means a conscious and voluntary abandonment of faith in the gospel of Jesus Christ.[10]

Apostasy is a rebellion against Christianity. Heresy is similar, as there are overlaps. Heresy involves holding on to false doctrine, such as believing that Jesus was just a created man (Arianism), or teaching that Jesus emptied His divinity when He came to earth (called the kenosis heresy).

It's possible that the false prophets of today don't know that they're teaching heresy, especially if they're defensive toward critics and refuse to compare their teachings to God's Word (the Bible). Spiritual blindness, as we'll discuss in this book, is a pervasive condition that keeps false prophets in the dark, which they mistakenly believe is the light.

I was necessarily humbled when I publicly denounced my prior teachings after Jesus saved me. How would you like to tell the whole world that you had been wrong? It was a painful but important process. That's when people started gossiping about my conversion, analyzing my actions, and speculating whether I was genuinely saved. Dozens of harsh videos and blogs criticized me and invented crazy stories about the "true motivation" for my conversion to Christianity.

It soon became public knowledge that my New Age publisher fired me and canceled my radio show, to the delight of critics who laughed that I deserved this punishment. I had to beg my publishers to stop printing and selling my old products, and then deal with several publishers who refused. I then experienced public backlash because others continued to sell my old books and cards. I had to tell people that my previous teachings were unbiblical and ask them to burn or toss out my old products so that they'd no longer be deceived by my old work.

Many of my friends and some family members stopped speaking to me because I was denouncing the New Age work with which they were involved. My social media posts against the New Age negatively impacted their income.

In Acts 16, we read about men who'd been making money from a slave girl who was possessed by an evil spirit that gave her psychic abilities. When the apostle Paul cast out this spirit and the girl lost her psychic abilities, the men were furious with Paul because of the lost income. Similarly, Paul was persecuted almost to death by men who made money from selling silver statues of pagan deities. When people stopped buying these statues after listening to Paul, he was hunted for retribution (Acts 19:23–41).

Mostly though, people seemed to interpret my denouncing as being "hate speech," when my entire motivation was love. I cared enough to warn people about the New Age leading to hell, and I risked losing everything and everyone to sound this warning. After all, no one had warned me about Christian Science being a false religion during the time that I was involved in it. And no one had taken the time to sit down with me and explain why New Age beliefs and practices are ungodly. I'm issuing the warnings that I wish someone would have given me during my fifty-eight years in deception.

Now that Jesus has saved my soul and given me a new heart and life, my memories of my formerly deceived views are fading. I'm writing this book to record the memories of my previous views before they completely diminish, to help you identify and avoid false prophets yourself.

In a way, this book is similar to a television interview I once watched, with a former house burglar giving his "insider secrets" so that we'd learn how to keep our homes safe from burglary. For example, he advised putting large dog bowls on the front porch, because when he was a robber, he'd avoid homes with big dogs.

Similarly, this book is my way of showing you the inside secrets of false prophets, including psychics, mediums, and channelers. This information can help you avoid being deceived by a false doctrine.

After spending a lifetime deceived by New Thought and New Age teachings, I came to Jesus and was saved at age fifty-eight. I'm excited to share my story, but first it's important to give you some background so that you'll see the significance of what happened.

ONE

The Woman at the Well

Two desires drove me as a New Age teacher: helping people and pursuing secret wisdom. My desire to help people started when I was young—my friends would tell me their problems, and I'd happily and dutifully listen. Nobody was surprised when I later majored in psychology and became a psychotherapist. I really wanted to help people, and I'd learned that listening was helpful to my friends and family. It seemed that people felt less lonely when someone took the time to listen.

After I graduated from Chapman University with an MA and BA in counseling psychology in 1988, I devoted myself to full-time work as a psychotherapist specializing in treating eating disorders and addictions. My first job was as an intake counselor at Palmdale Hospital in Southern California. I'd meet with people who were considering inpatient care to detox and receive therapeutic treatment for their addictions. My job was to ask them questions about their substance abuse habits and their family background. Once they were admitted to the hospital, I'd spend time with them, including accompanying them to on-site 12-step meetings.

1

My next job was working with eating-disordered clients at an out-patient psychiatric clinic. My boss was a psychiatrist who sat behind a giant wooden desk, listening to his patients and then sending them home with psychotropic drug prescriptions. Sometimes the doctor would take me on his inpatient hospital rounds, including watching him give electroshocks to a woman who'd been traumatized from being kidnapped and raped. As I watched the doctor place paddles on her head and she convulsed on the gurney, I knew there had to be another way besides shocks or drugs to deal with post-traumatic issues.

My clients at the clinic were mostly women who'd been abused as children. They were trying to fill their emptiness and angst through overeating. Some of the women sought admiration for their thin bodies through restrictive dieting. I understood. Throughout my life I've struggled with "daddy issues," having been raised by a father who is all logic and no emotions. Dad (who presently lives with me, my mother, my husband, and my mother-in-law) was an only child who became an aerospace engineer. In the navy, he worked on an aircraft carrier. He identifies himself as a highly sensitive empath, and he prefers to be holed up in his home office, watching YouTube videos about exotic cars. He's always had a passion for vintage airplanes, model airplanes, and automobiles. Dad once made a scrapbook of his life, and it's 90 percent pictures of the cars he's owned since adolescence. Even his wedding-day photos emphasize the car that he and Mom owned at the time.

I always felt hungry for Dad's love, attention, and approval. To Dad, though, love was shown by being a faithful family provider. I didn't realize at the time that our heavenly Father God provides for all our needs, including our need to feel cared for and loved. Instead, I began a lifelong pattern of looking outside myself for love and approval. I'd "fall in love" quickly and commit to relationships with guys instead of taking the time to first get to know them. I'd jump in under an idealized fantasy that the person would fulfill my love needs.

I got quickly involved in inappropriate relationships with drug addicts and alcoholics who seemed to "need" my emotional and financial help. I was always the sole provider in these relationships. The strain resulted in a string of painful breakups, as I searched for love through people instead of through God. With my stony pre-salvation heart, I wasn't capable of fully loving another. So even if the most loving man had been in my life at that time, I couldn't have appreciated his love. I was unknowingly hungry for the love that only God can give.

I'd followed all the New Age prescriptions for healthy, happy living: I'd done yoga for twenty years, cleared my chakras, carefully spoken only positive words, avoided signing contracts during Mercury retrograde, saged and feng shuied my home, consulted my angel cards, said positive affirmations, meditated daily, and cleared my crystals during the full moon. The New Age, for all its promises, could not save me. Only Jesus could.

When Jesus saved me, I was like the woman at the well, who had continually thirsted for love but couldn't find it. Jesus offered her, and all of us, living water. When the woman asked Jesus about the living water, He explained, "Whoever drinks of the water that I will give him will never be thirsty again. The water that I will give him will become in him a spring of water welling up to eternal life" (John 4:14). In other words, Jesus quenches our thirst for love, because He offers a love that fills our hearts in a way no mortal relationship can.

When I was a child, our family lived on a very tight budget in expensive Southern California. Dad had quit his aerospace engineering job to stay home and write books about his passion for balsa, rubber band–powered model airplanes and draw blueprints for them. It sounds obscure, and it was! Yet Dad managed to make enough income to provide for us all, even if it meant scrimping.

We economized by buying discounted clothing. This guaranteed that I always wore out-of-style clothes, which personally didn't concern me except that the other girls in my Southern California school openly judged anyone who had "dorky" (their term for unfashionable) clothing or hairstyles. The pressure in Southern California to stay up with the latest fashions was, and continues to be, enormous. It encourages materialism and superficiality. Just as I didn't know that I was raised in a false gospel, I also didn't know that an obsession with fashion is an idolatrous distraction from the true gospel. Anything that takes our focus away from Jesus becomes an idol. Anything that promotes self-glory over God-glory is an idol.

Anyway, my heart hungered for love, and the popular kids at school avoided me because of my humble clothing. I know that sounds superficial, but Southern California has earned that reputation for a reason. Maybe you can relate to this: I was an outcast, the weird kid at the edge of the school playground. Part of the reason was the Christian Science vocabulary I was raised with. We used jargon like "manifestation" before the New Age movement popularized that term.

Our religion also barred us from taking health or science classes in school, because we believed that if you learned about an illness, you'd "manifest" that illness. Christian Science is big into mind control. You're not allowed to think or say anything negative, because negativity could result in manifesting a negative life circumstance. This belief folded me right into the New Age, which holds an identical belief. While the Bible does emphasize the benefits of positive thinking (Proverbs 23:7 NKJV; Philippians 4:6–8), to give credit to human thought over God's sovereignty is blasphemy. Instead of taking health and science classes in school, I took art electives. I may as well have had a sign hanging from my back announcing that I was an oddball.

I had two close girlfriends in childhood, Silvia and Anita, who seemed to love and accept me despite my being a social outcast. We are still close friends to this day.

Anita was tall, model-thin, very popular, and she came from an affluent family. One summer evening, Anita invited me to an upscale party at a friend's house. We were escorted into her friend's bedroom, where the friend opened her closet to display a dazzling array of gorgeous, fashionable clothing. It was the 1970s, so the popular fashions then were India block prints popularized by the Beatles' 1968 sojourn to Mahesh Yogi's Transcendental Meditation course in Rishikesh, and romantic lacy maxi dresses by Gunne Sax and Jessica McClintock.

When I saw that closet full of dreamy, ethereal fabrics, I figured that if I could have clothing like that, the kids at school would accept me. I wasn't jealous or coveting; I was just seeking the secret to feeling loved. I didn't yet realize that *only* Jesus could provide the love I was seeking.

After that party, I became obsessed with acquiring the latest fashions. To make money for clothes, I babysat, walked dogs, and cleaned our neighbors' houses. This obsession continued through adulthood, including my time as a New Age teacher in the public eye. My childhood insecurities about what to wear would come flooding back, so I'd overcompensate by buying expensive clothing to wear onstage and on television. For a while, I was able to deduct them on my taxes as work uniforms, but then the tax laws changed and it was just me spending way too much money on fancy designer dresses.

After I was saved, I prayed to understand why I was so obsessed with clothing, particularly 1970s-style dresses. That's when I realized that I was trying to impress those girls from high school who had the beautiful clothing closets. And the illogic hit me! Even if I had the most amazing 1970s dress on, those girls would've moved on from that style, and I still wouldn't be accepted. Soon after that, I donated and sold most of those clothes and learned how to wear modest and inexpensive clothing with grace. Today I buy my clothes at charity thrift stores, discount department stores, or from eBay. After almost six decades of seeking love and approval from people, I've finally learned that only Jesus can quench our thirst for love.

5

The Desire for Secret Wisdom

I mentioned that there were two desires that drove me toward the New Age. The first was a desire to help people, and the second was a desire for secret wisdom, as my family's religion wasn't answering my questions. Since the age of twelve, I'd wondered about mortality and the afterlife. I remember going into the Christian Science Reading Room where my mom volunteered and searching for a book about death and the afterlife. When I couldn't find anything, I asked Mom for this material. She promptly told me that I was too young to worry about such matters.

I somehow became convinced that the answers must be in some old book, so I started to read turn-of-the-century spiritual books. That was the era of the 1800s, when Phineas Quimby was giving seminars on mesmerism (hypnosis) and mental healing. Quimby also wrote books, such as *Science of Man*, teaching that disease stems from erroneous beliefs.[1]

Among Quimby's students were the men and women who turned his work into the heretical Christian Science, Religious Science, Divine Science, and Unity religions. Quimby taught that Jesus was a created being whom we could learn from for the purposes of "manifesting" (cocreating with God) health and wealth.

When Mary Baker Eddy started the Christian Science religion and wrote the book she claimed explained the Bible, *Science and Health with Key to the Scriptures*, Quimby's son and others accused her of plagiarism. When comparing Quimby's and Eddy's books side by side, you can see the similarities. The editor of Eddy's book, a retired Unitarian minister, later revealed his part in the plagiarism scheme in the pamphlet *How Rev. Wiggin Rewrote Mrs. Eddy's Book*.[2] You can also read about the time line of Quimby influencing Eddy in *The Quimby Manuscripts* by Horatio W. Dresser, which is now a free publication on many websites.

In addition to plagiarism, I believe the similarities between Quimby's and Eddy's book came from demonic influences that caused both people to teach heresies and a false gospel.

Many people think that the originator of the Word-Faith movement, Essek William "E. W." Kenyon, was a student of Phineas Quimby's, and so he received the same instruction as Mary Baker Eddy. Although Kenyon was alive during Quimby's era, biblical apologist Robert Bowman claims that Kenyon was not Quimby's student, but that he did study and was influenced by metaphysical teachings. Kenyon may have also been impressed by the large congregations at Christian Science churches during that era of its popularity when he said, "Christian Science could not have grown to the place where it is dominating many of our large cities unless there had been a demand in the heart of the people for a supernatural religion."[3]

The similarities between Christian Science, which claims that you can speak and think the right words and reveal health, and Word-Faith, which claims that you can speak the right words and claim wealth, show common grounds. Both Kenyon and Eddy say that their teachings came from revelation knowledge.[4] Again, I believe this is because the devil is the same author of all false teachings. Every false prophecy reflects the promises the serpent said to Eve in the garden (Genesis 3).

While it's true that our words and our prayers affect our outcomes, it's essential to ensure that we're only praying for God's will to be done. False prophets teach that you can conjure whatever your heart desires, which is a recipe for living against God's will. My life in the New Age is a testimony to the disasters that occur when you follow your own will instead of God's will.

The tentacles of Christian Science influenced my New Age teachings and other New Age teachers as well. Helen Schucman, the author of *A Course in Miracles*, was raised by a mother who dabbled in Christian Science and Unity, which both share the same Phineas

Quimby roots. Schucman's book is often called "the New Age bible," and it has sold more than three million copies worldwide according to its publisher. Popular New Age teacher Louise Hay, who was my publisher for twenty-five years, also told me that she was influenced by her mother's Christian Science beliefs. No wonder the tentacles of Christian Science heresy have become so entangled in church and secular practices today! The devil worked undercover through New Age teachers to spread his anti-gospel message.

What hooked many of us into Christian Science were the apparent demonstrations of spiritual healings. My family was lower middle class after my father quit his aerospace engineering job in order to create a home-based business selling model airplane plans and books. We didn't have enough money to pay for doctor's appointments. Mom would pray over our cuts, bruises, and illnesses, and it seemed as if we healed quickly. Each Wednesday night, we'd go to the church's testimonial meetings and hear people discuss their healings.

Similarly, in the New Age, people claim to be healed during Reiki energy sessions, shamanic retreats, and other metaphysical types of treatments. I recently asked discernment researcher and author Justin Peters how it was possible for people to be spiritually healed from apostate sources. Both Peters and I believe that God still miraculously heals. However, Peters, who has suffered from cerebral palsy his whole life, initially went to faith healers until he started to see the gimmicks in faith-healing shows. The faith healers never approached people in wheelchairs, like Peters, and he soon realized these shows were fabricated. Later in seminary, Peters wrote his thesis on the topic of faith healing. My point is that he knows a lot about the topic.

Peters told me that two types of healing result from apostate sources, such as Christian Science and Reiki energy:

- **Psychosomatic healing.** This is a temporary condition where the adrenaline from being excited about possibly receiving a healing gives the appearance of a healing or a momentary masking of the pain. This is where someone believes that he or she is healed and feels better in the euphoria of the moment. Doctors have given people sugar pills (placebos) and convinced them the pills would lead to wellness, which they did.

- **Demonic influences.** Peters explained that demons can create sickness or cause injuries and then lead the sick person to a false teacher who seems to heal, so that the person is then drawn away from the gospel and toward a false teaching.[5]

How I wish I could've talked with Justin Peters years ago! Instead, I scoured used bookstores for secret wisdom, while my Bible containing all the answers sat unread on my shelf. Except for the "weekly lessons" in Christian Science, which assigned us out-of-context verses to read along with commentary by Mary Baker Eddy, I hadn't read the Bible. What I had read were plenty of New Thought books that tried to blend Christianity with mystical motivational inspiration by such authors as Norman Vincent Peale and Emmet Fox.

I knew some Bible stories without realizing how they fit in with the gospel. I was biblically illiterate but would have argued with anyone who called me that back then. Because I'd skimmed passages from Genesis through Revelation in the Christian Science weekly lessons, I *felt* as if I'd read the entire Bible. But feeling and actually reading the Bible are two different things.

After Jesus saved me out of the New Age, I threw away hundreds of books I'd collected over the years. Each book had promised to show me the truth and reveal hidden secrets, and I'd fallen for these lies just as Eve fell for the serpent's lies in the garden.

The promise of gaining secret wisdom was the first lie ever told. God had clearly warned Adam not to eat of the tree of the knowledge of good and evil, or he would surely die (Genesis 2:16–17). Adam shared this commandment with Eve; however, she added an extra twist to the commandment when she told the serpent that they were not allowed to touch the tree. That wasn't God's command.

The serpent took advantage of Eve's soft knowledge of God's word, and he challenged her: "Are you really sure that's what God said? Did He actually say that? . . . Surely you won't really die! God only said that because He knows you'll gain extra knowledge if you eat from that tree" (Genesis 3:1, 4–5, paraphrased).

Eve was willing to defy God in order to gain secret wisdom. Perhaps she wasn't consciously disobeying God, but allowing herself to be persuaded that God didn't really mean what He said. The serpent was a crafty salesman who enticed Eve with a conspiracy theory that God was hiding secret wisdom from her and Adam. So, Eve took matters into her own hands to get the promised prize of hidden wisdom.

In a similar way, I was unknowingly disobeying God in my quest for secret wisdom. I'd been raised on twisted Scripture and watered-down, heretical teachings that came straight from the serpent. I also believed that the government, the Vatican, or "someone" had hidden the universal truth from us ordinary people. I wanted to beat the system and find that truth.

I scoured used bookstores and attended classes on Eastern mysticism, metaphysics, spiritual healing, psychic development, Egyptology, Hermetics, and other "forbidden" teachings. I rationalized that I was acquiring this knowledge for the purpose of helping people. I avoided material that seemed dark and frightening, such as witchcraft, Wicca, or sorcery. Technically, though, I was crossing over into these areas with my studies, especially when I began taking mediumship classes. Somehow I rationalized that I was safe as long as I didn't get into witchcraft.

Please keep in mind that I hadn't yet read or heard the biblical laws prohibiting witchcraft, sorcery, divination, mediumship, or interpreting omens. When the Holy Spirit opened my eyes to these Scripture passages, everything changed for me. More on that story later, though.

At that time, I was just following what interested me and avoiding what frightened me. Harry Potter books and movies, pentagrams, and witchcraft in general frightened me, so I avoided those.

I earned certificates for various forms of spiritual healing and divination. My obsession with gaining secret, hidden knowledge also included a desire to peek into the future. This appetite arose from my desire to control the future. I thought that if I could foresee what would happen, then I could avoid, or prepare for, painful situations. Instead of trusting God, I was leaning on my own understanding.

TWO

Testing the Spirits

Sometime around 1997, I had a vivid dream about my grandma Pearl. She'd passed away, and it seemed as though she was speaking to me from heaven. In this dream, Grandma walked me through a house filled with tapestry-upholstered wooden furniture, like something you'd see in a medieval castle. This home sat on a hill and overlooked the ocean through large picture windows. My grandma asked me if I wanted this home and furniture, and like a little girl whose grandmother offers a dollhouse, I clapped my hands in the dream and said, "Yes!" Grandma acknowledged my desire and said, "Okay then. You'll need to study Pythagoras." She conveyed that if I were to study Pythagoras, I'd have that oceanfront home with the castle-like furniture.

Then I woke up. "Pythagoras?" I said aloud. "You mean like the 'triangle guy' from high school algebra class?" I had no idea how to "study Pythagoras," so I asked a new friend of mine, who happily loaded my arms with books about the Pythagorean theorem and such. I felt as if I was on an archaeological dig searching for buried treasure. What exactly I was seeking, I didn't know. Now, though, I realize that a demon had masqueraded as my grandma Pearl, and reeled me in like a fish eager to take the bait of ambitious desires.

The apostle John taught us how to deal with situations like my dreams by testing the spirits:

> Beloved, do not believe every spirit, but test the spirits to see whether they are from God, for many false prophets have gone out into the world. By this you know the Spirit of God: every spirit that confesses that Jesus Christ has come in the flesh is from God, and every spirit that does not confess Jesus is not from God. This is the spirit of the antichrist, which you heard was coming and now is in the world already. (1 John 4:1–3)

Using the apostle John's criterion, the spirit in my dream failed the test. First, the spirit posing as my grandma did not point me to Jesus and did not confess Jesus. My grandma was a Christian who had attended a Presbyterian church, so I would've expected her to say something about God or Jesus in heaven, or at least point me to a Christian teacher. Instead, the spirit appearing in my dream pointed me to an unbiblical pagan teacher, Pythagoras.

When a spirit appears in a dream through another person's words, or an intuitive impulse, we can test whether the message confesses that Jesus came to earth in the flesh from God. Using that criterion, I could've immediately seen the demonic nature of Mary Baker Eddy's Christian Science teachings and the New Age teachings about a false Jesus or no Jesus at all.

We must always be discerning to notice whether a message leads us toward or away from God, Jesus, and the Bible. False spirits will say that they're a substitute for the Bible, because they know that if you read the Bible you will follow God instead of the false spirit. That's why New Age teachings speak vigilantly against the Bible.

Before Jesus saved me and my eyes were opened to this realization, though, I was fooled by the spirit impersonating my grandma in the dream. Like falling for those spam phone calls or emails that are trying to trick you, I fell for the dream and immersed myself in studying Pythagoras's theories about mathematics and the universe.

Somehow the rabbit trail of researching Pythagoras led me to Egyptian mysticism and numerology, which eventually led me to studying tarot—as in tarot cards. *I know, I know!* They're horribly demonic, yet the stew I was in was on a long, slow boil, and I hadn't yet realized that I was in its caldron. I still believed I was in charge, and that I'd attracted this situation through positive thinking and affirmations. *I can handle this*, I told myself. Yeah, sure.

After becoming a Christian, my intuition seriously changed. I still have occasional dreams that are beyond chance. For example, I dreamed that my granddaughter Gena needed some new shoes. The next morning when I contacted her, Gena was so surprised to hear about my dreams. "My shoe just broke yesterday!" she exclaimed. So I gave her mother some money to get a replacement pair of shoes for Gena.

Now when I have an intuitive experience, I don't try to analyze it, but instead trust in God's mysteries. I lay the intuitive thought, dream, or feeling at the foot of the cross. That way, I'm not tempted to use the intuition as an idol, like a substitute for following God's guidance in the Bible.

Was that dream a message from God or an angel? After all, the Bible is filled with stories of prophetic dreams. I don't believe it was special divine revelation from God or an angel, though. Justin Peters helped me to understand this point when I recently interviewed him on my YouTube channel. He explained that every word from God carries equal weight and importance. Any message that comes from God would be the equivalent of, for example, John 3:16. If God continued to give special revelation, then the Bible would need to stay open to additions. Yet the Bible's canon is closed because everything has been said. All the Bible's prophecies about the coming Messiah have been fulfilled, and the final prophecies of end times are unfolding.

We can also compare my dream to Scripture, to see if there's anything similar. There's not. So, what was the source of my dream about my granddaughter's shoes? I believe that Gena was praying about her shoes and that God uses other people—in this case, me, her grandmother—to answer prayers.

Before I was saved, though, I would have credited this dream to any number of sources: an angel, an ancestor, or even Gena's soul speaking to my soul. Ironically, I would not have considered that God would speak to me directly even back then.

You see, my view of God was that He was the "energy of love," an impersonal and universal love mixed with all-knowing, divine wisdom. In Christian Science, I'd been taught that God was "Divine Mind." As a child, I pictured this mind as a giant brain in the sky. How can you feel love or closeness to a brain? How can you know, love, or trust "an energy"? One of the reasons I didn't trust God is because I didn't know Him until I started studying the Bible, which is where He reveals Himself to humanity.

I had such an incomplete viewpoint of the attributes of God back then! That's one of many reasons we all need to read the entire Bible, because God reveals Himself through Scripture. We can only see how consistent God is when we take the time to read the entire Bible from Genesis 1 through Revelation 22. Back then, I only read bits of the Bible here and there. Well, how could I fully understand any book by only reading parts? We'd miss the continuity, the theme, the nuances, and the details. We can't skim or cherry-pick the Bible and hope to know God.

What I didn't realize was that God's love is an attribute under the umbrella of His holiness. The late theologian R. C. Sproul wrote in his classic book *The Holiness of God*:

The primary meaning of holy is "separate." It comes from an ancient word that means "to cut," or "to separate." . . . Perhaps even more accurate would be the phrase, "a cut above something." . . . God's holiness is more than just separateness. His holiness is also transcendent. . . . It is defined as "exceeding usual limits." . . . Transcendence describes God in His consuming majesty, His exalted loftiness. It points to the infinite distance that separates Him from every creature. . . . When the Bible calls God holy, it means primarily that God is transcendentally separate. He is so far above and beyond us that He seems totally foreign to us. To be holy is to be "other," to be different in a special way.[1]

Because of God's purity, He has no ability to tolerate impurity. In other words, God and sin cannot coexist. That's why Adam and Eve were kicked out of the garden after they disobeyed God. Without Jesus, no one can be in the presence of God, because we've all inherited the rebellious and willful nature of our ancestors. Just watch a three-year-old for an hour, and you'll see humanity's inherently headstrong nature. In the Bible, God calls this trait being "stiff-necked." That term refers to a horse that can't be steered because it ignores the reins and direction of its rider. In the same way, we all jump ahead of God and want to steer ourselves.

In the New Age, my beliefs about God were:

- **Pantheism** is the belief that God *is* all things. The universe and all life are connected in the total reality of God. Thus, humans, animals, plants, and all physical matter are seen as equal and "all is one"; therefore, all is deity.[2] I'm embarrassed to say that I once held this belief, which led me to see all humans as gods and goddesses in training. Yet, the biblical teaching of omnipresence means that God is everywhere, not *in* everything. There's an equally important biblical doctrine that God is separate from His creation. God is the Creator, not the creation. That's why Romans 1 denounces worshiping the creation instead of the Creator.

- **Panentheism** teaches that God is *in* all things, and that the universe and all matter is contained within God. I adopted this belief while studying Egyptian Hermetics, which teaches that the whole world is contained within God's mind and coined the phrase "as above, so below." Panentheism also holds to the heretical view that God is "learning" through our experiences.

What woke me out of these false viewpoints was studying one of the oldest books of the Bible: Job. If you haven't yet read the book of Job, let me highly recommend it to you. In summary, God allows Satan to have limited access to the righteous man Job. Satan takes away everything from Job: his family, home, and his health. Yet through this crisis, Job remains steadfast in his faith in God.

Job's friends argue that he must've sinned to warrant this severe punishment. Job argues back that he's innocent, but he also wants to talk to God and get some answers. And that's what happens! God shows up and reveals His true nature and character to Job! God's dialogue in Job chapters 38 through 41 is what awakened me out of pantheism and panentheism.

God asked Job (and all of us) whether we were capable of creating the universe: "Where were you when I laid the foundation of the earth?" and "Have you commanded the morning since your days began?" and "Can you lift up your voice to the clouds, that a flood of waters may cover you? Can you send forth lightnings?" (Job 38:4, 12, 34–35).

For four chapters, God outlines everything He can do that we can't do. In the most beautifully therapeutic way, reading these chapters burst my illusion that I was a "cocreator with God," a common phrase in the New Age. And let me tell you that it was a huge relief to realize that I wasn't in charge of the universe, as I'd mistakenly believed! God is in charge, which I'm so happy to finally know.

We'll all stand before God on Judgment Day and be held accountable for everything we said and did (gulp!). We've all broken the Ten Commandments, so we will all stand guilty before Him. God is loving and merciful, but He's also a judge of justice. Just as a courthouse judge can't overlook a car thief or a burglar, so, too, God can't overlook our years of using His name in vain, practicing idolatry, slandering our neighbor, having lustful thoughts, dishonoring our parents, and so forth. Sinful behavior always has consequences.

This isn't an appeal to legalism, however. We can't earn our way into heaven through good behavior. First, it's not possible to be good all the time as God defines "good." The Bible says that only Jesus was sinless (2 Corinthians 5:21; Hebrews 4:15; 1 Peter 2:22). Jesus took the punishment on the cross that we deserved because of our sins.

It took me fifty-eight years to understand this, though. During those years of deception, I didn't know what the word *salvation* meant. I held the universalist and pluralistic heretical beliefs that everyone goes to heaven. I got that idea from our Christian Science religion, which only emphasized God's love and not His holiness. In that religion, a loving God would automatically forgive everyone and allow them into heaven.

In the New Age, we'd focus on the accounts of people who claimed to have near-death experiences of heaven. They weren't Christian, yet they said they were welcomed into heaven along with other non-Christians. They reported that in their near-death experience, all was forgiven and everything was about tolerance and universal love.

Doesn't that sound heavenly? Wouldn't that be wonderful if it were true? Except it's not. The devil uses tricks such as this to deceptively calm people into believing that you can do whatever you want and still be accepted into heaven.

In the New Age, we also didn't focus on the equal number of

people who said they had near-death experiences of hell. Those folks were shown the gates of hell, and each described the same scenario of ear-shattering screams from souls in constant agony as they were cruelly tortured by merciless demons. After their hellish near-death experience, they invariably turned to Jesus and committed to the straight-and-narrow path.

Were these near-death experiences delusions from oxygen-starved, dying brains, or demonically inspired hallucinations? Or were they really shown glimpses of the afterlife? Again, we must compare everything to Scripture to avoid veering off into false teachings.

The Bible gives us clear teachings about hell, including Jesus' frequent references to it. The story Jesus taught of the rich man in hell is frightening and convicting in important ways.

In Luke 16, we read that the Pharisees were ridiculing Jesus because of His teachings about the right use of money. The Bible says that the Pharisees "were lovers of money" (v. 14). Jesus pulled out all the stops when telling this next story. Normally, Jesus would tell parables as examples of the principles He taught. But in this story, Jesus used real names and circumstances. This story is a more-than-real warning to the Pharisees, and to us today. It's the story of a rich man who had every earthly desire, yet he wasn't saved, so when he died, he was cast into Hades. In contrast to the rich man, a poor man named Lazarus (no relation to the Lazarus whom Jesus raised from the dead) suffered during his earthly life and went to heaven after death. This isn't a story about riches being evil and poverty being pious. It's about the love of money and the wrong use of money:

> "There was a rich man who was clothed in purple and fine linen and who feasted sumptuously every day. And at his gate was laid a poor man named Lazarus, covered with sores, who desired to be fed with what fell from the rich man's table. Moreover, even the dogs came and licked his sores. The poor man died and was carried by

the angels to Abraham's side. The rich man also died and was buried, and in Hades, being in torment, he lifted up his eyes and saw Abraham far off and Lazarus at his side. And he called out, 'Father Abraham, have mercy on me, and send Lazarus to dip the end of his finger in water and cool my tongue, for I am in anguish in this flame.' But Abraham said, 'Child, remember that you in your lifetime received your good things, and Lazarus in like manner bad things; but now he is comforted here, and you are in anguish. And besides all this, between us and you a great chasm has been fixed, in order that those who would pass from here to you may not be able, and none may cross from there to us.' And he said, 'Then I beg you, father, to send him to my father's house—for I have five brothers—so that he may warn them, lest they also come into this place of torment.' But Abraham said, 'They have Moses and the Prophets; let them hear them.' And he said, 'No, father Abraham, but if someone goes to them from the dead, they will repent.' He said to him, 'If they do not hear Moses and the Prophets, neither will they be convinced if someone should rise from the dead.'"
(Luke 16:19–31)

This story makes me shudder! After we die, it's too late for repentance. Theologian and author Warren Wiersbe wrote that this story "refutes so-called 'soul-sleep,' for both the rich man and Lazarus were conscious, one enjoying comfort and the other suffering torment. It is a solemn thing to ponder one's eternal destiny and realize the reality of divine punishment."[3]

I'd never worried *where* I'd spend eternity, because New Age teachings always reassured us that we all go to heaven. One of the most sobering passages in the Bible is where Jesus warns what will happen to people who don't follow Him, or who follow a false Jesus instead of the real Jesus.

Jesus said in Matthew 7:21–23: "Not everyone who says to me,

'Lord, Lord,' will enter the kingdom of heaven, but the one who does the will of my Father who is in heaven. On that day many will say to me, 'Lord, Lord, did we not prophesy in your name, and cast out demons in your name, and do many mighty works in your name?' And then will I declare to them, 'I never knew you; depart from me, you workers of lawlessness.'"

I can't even imagine standing before Jesus and because you'd followed a false Jesus, the real Jesus says that He doesn't know who you are. Then, you're cast off into utter darkness—into hell. The thought is horrifying!

How do you get to know the real Jesus? By reading Jesus' words in the Bible, by praying to get closer to Him, by learning about Him, thinking about Him, and obeying Him. Jesus said, "If anyone loves me, he will keep my word, and my Father will love him, and we will come to him and make our home with him" (John 14:23).

Many people argue: But it's not fair that God sends anyone to hell! Actually, it's not fair that God sends anyone to heaven, considering that we've all sinned (Romans 3:23). If there was ever a person besides Jesus who was perfectly obedient, that person would go to heaven. But there's not, because our human nature wants to rebel.

The only way for a sinful person to enter heaven is to go through Jesus. The Bible tells us that our heavenly Father God created everything through Jesus (John 1:1–18; Colossians 1:15–19). When Jesus said, "I am the way, and the truth, and the life. No one comes to the Father except through me" (John 14:6), He was giving us the road map to heaven. At the end of our lives, when our sins are judged, we need Jesus alongside us telling Father God that our sins have been forgiven by Jesus' work on the cross.

But what about people who've never heard about Jesus? What about people of other religions? Or indigenous people who have no access to the Bible? That's why Jesus commissioned all believers to share the gospel to all people of all nations (Matthew 28:16–20).

"There is no hell," according to New Thought and New Age teachings. It's just a myth perpetuated by the church who wants to scare you into submission. "Hell is what you make of your life here on earth," says the false Christ. Well, that's what I used to believe, and I almost ended up in hell for eternity—not as punishment for holding these false beliefs, but because I didn't trust the real Jesus, who spoke about hell more than anyone else in the Bible. I trust Jesus and the Bible more than I trust New Age and New Thought teachers, especially when it comes to my eternal destination. Eternity is a long, long time to figure out that you followed the wrong teacher.

Theologian Charles Spurgeon demonstrated the right use of money. During his lifetime in the 1800s of writing bestselling books, Spurgeon earned more than $26 million in today's currency. Yet he died poor because he spent that money to help others through donations, funding the school expenses of future pastors, funding additions to his church, and founding two orphanages.[4]

One of the ways to detect a false prophet is the way they handle money: how they spend it, and whether they try to manipulate, guilt, falsely promise, or cajole money from followers. If a religious leader or spiritual teacher implies that you will receive God's favor in exchange for your donation to their ministry, run the other way, get out your Bible, and start studying Scripture daily. God never requires us to donate money to a ministry in order to gain His favor!

Although John Charles "J. C." Ryle came from an affluent family and he excelled at sports, he was aware at a young age that all was not well with his soul. When he was afflicted with a serious chest infection, J. C. turned to his Bible and prayer. Soon after, at church, he heard the pastor read Ephesians 2:8, "For by grace you have been saved through faith. And this is not your own doing; it is the gift of God" and felt that the Lord was speaking directly to his soul with this verse. J. C. said that he was saved that day through hearing the Word of God. He later became an Anglican bishop in Liverpool, England,

and wrote a series of commentary books about the Gospels, according to Banner of Truth Publishers, who now reprints his books.

J. C. Ryle knew from experience that it's vital for us all to study the Bible. He wrote:

> What is the best safe-guard against false teaching? Beyond all doubt the regular study of the word of God, with prayer for the teaching of the Holy Spirit. The Bible was given to be a lamp to our feet and a light to our path (Psalm 119:105). The man who reads it aright will never be allowed greatly to err. It is neglect of the Bible which makes so many a prey to the first false teacher whom they hear. . . . The world, the devil, and the flesh, are not the only dangers in the way of the Christian. There remains another yet, and that is the "false prophet," the wolf in sheep's clothing. Happy is he who prays over his Bible and knows the difference between truth and error in religion! There is a difference, and we are meant to know it, and use our knowledge.[5]

THREE

Sin Was a Four-Letter Word

For almost six decades of following a false Jesus and false teachers, I remained unsaved. If I'd died during that time, I would've certainly gone straight to hell for eternity. I was following a false Christ and heretical beliefs instead of the true Jesus and the true gospel.

As a result, I hadn't repented because I didn't think I was doing anything from which I needed to repent. My childhood religion and the New Age assured me that I was "perfect, whole, and complete." We were encouraged to affirm that phrase whenever we felt bad about ourselves, which was often since we were unknowingly living without the true Jesus.

A lot of us in the New Age felt bad about ourselves because we suffered from symptoms of post-traumatic incidents (more about that topic later). But mostly, we felt bad about ourselves from the enormous pressure of holding on to guilt instead of repenting, trying to run our own lives instead of surrendering to God, following spirit guides instead of the King of kings Jesus, and trying to fill our hearts with things, people, or accomplishments instead of the love of God.

Many New Agers like me had "daddy issues" that repelled them from what they perceived as the patriarchy of Christianity. They turned to spirituality that seemed softer and more feminine, like angel and goddess worship. While those paths may seem to offer a gentler approach for a traumatized person, I learned from personal experience that they actually lead to more pain, loneliness, and the weight of guilt and shame.

I'd heard the word *sin* plenty of times but didn't understand its meaning. Instead of using the word *sin*, Christian Science and the New Age twisted Genesis 1:26, that we were made in God's image, and claimed that humans are eternally divine. We of course knew of the garden of Eden but thought it was metaphorical or even mythical.

In 2016, my husband, Michael, and I began attending a Pentecostal church where the pastor led the congregation through the "sinner's prayer" at monthly communion. He'd also remind us churchgoers, "You know that we're all sinners, right?" I'd stare at the pastor, not understanding what he was talking about. If someone called me a sinner, I equated this with saying, "You're a bad person." Why was the pastor calling himself and his congregation bad people?

The word *sin* was like a four-letter curse word to me, because it seemed so judgmental and negative. Christian Science and the New Age had drilled into my head to always stay positive. Deny the reality of death, sin, and disease. Never think or say anything negative about yourself, or something horrible could happen as a result. And that horrible occurrence would be all your fault because you attracted it with your negativity.

If the New Age had ten commandments, the first would be "Thou shalt always be positive." Looking back, I can see that I was terrified of my own thoughts creating a bad situation. I never allowed myself to think about anything sad or frightening. I lived like an ostrich most of my life, which isn't a good way to confront life's inevitable challenges. Instead of working through conflicts in relationships, I'd leave. Instead of dealing with financial problems, I'd ignore them. I thought problems would magically disappear if I pretended they weren't there.

I always thought of myself as a Christian. I used some Christian terminology in my books and speeches, because I was raised with such terms mixed in with metaphysical and New Age jargon. Among the New Age teachers, I was one of the few who talked about God, Jesus, the Holy Spirit, and angels. Of course, I spoke of them in heretical and unbiblical ways, but unless someone had read the Bible, none of us realized this. Now that I've read the entire Bible several times, I'm grieved by the contrast between what I once believed and taught and what Scripture actually says.

I was unwittingly teaching a New Age form of Gnosticism, which is the belief that God is unknowable, so you'd better save yourself through mystical experiences of receiving special knowledge (gnosis). Gnostics also hold the heretical belief that Jesus came to earth as a spirit, that He didn't suffer on the cross.[1]

The Gnostic worship of angels was rampant when Paul wrote this warning to the Colossians: "Don't let anyone condemn you by insisting on pious self-denial or the worship of angels, saying they have had visions about these things. Their sinful minds have made them proud, and they are not connected to Christ, the head of the body" (Colossians 2:18–19 NLT). The Gnostics practiced and taught the same methods that I did, of turning to the angels for guidance instead of to God. The Gnostics were prideful that they'd received visions, which were likely whatever popped into their minds.

Although I called myself a Christian, I thought of born-again Christians as being different from me. I judged them as "fear-based," which is a New Age term for someone who operates out of fear, guilt, and negativity. I also thought their manner of dress was boringly conservative.

It wasn't until I read Deuteronomy 18:10–12 that I realized the psychic and divination work I'd been doing was sinful. That's when the realization broke me: I was a sinner whose actions were an abomination to God. I'll tell you more about this soon.

The important point right now is that until I realized I was a sinner, I didn't know that I needed a Savior. I needed to be humbled and realize that I couldn't save myself. I wasn't the good person I thought I was.

Now, we're not saved by the action of repentance. We repent *because* we are saved. Our heart before salvation is hardened and worldly, and we don't care whether we're rebelling against God. Or maybe we do care, but we don't know that we're rebelling because we haven't studied the Bible. That was me, as a biblically illiterate person who was unaware that I was in rebellion against God and hurting myself and others in the process.

FOUR

Rock-Star Lifestyle

I'd worked really hard to become the bestselling New Age author at the top New Age publishing house. For two decades, I'd sat at my computer, writing books instead of going to the movies or parties. Eventually, I made enough money to have an oceanfront home that looked eerily similar to the house I'd seen in my dream with Grandma Pearl. Instead of enjoying the beach below my home, however, I sat writing while looking at the people on the beach who seemed to be having fun. After all, I had to make enough money to pay the expenses that all my "manifesting" work had incurred, including the five-figure monthly mortgage payment. If I'd thought about this irony, I might have realized that "the law of attraction," which the New Age teaches, doesn't actually work. You may "attract" your desires, but someone's got to pay for them—which is what I was doing instead of enjoying my oceanfront house or the other goodies that I'd "manifested."

At the time, my ambition seemed benevolent and unselfish. I genuinely believed that I was helping people and giving them messages from God's angels. I even felt altruistic, like a martyr denying myself pleasure in order to bring the latest messages to people in my books, audios, videos, seminars, and cards. I was a self-appointed prophetess on a mission.

Little did I realize that the devil was behind this part of my life. That old serpent was still telling the same old lies of promising secret hidden wisdom, and I'd fallen for it. Had I taken the time to study the entire Bible, I would have read, "And no wonder, for even Satan disguises himself as an angel of light" (2 Corinthians 11:14).

Now I also realize how the devil takes advantage of ambitious people, especially those who feel unloved and lonely, as I did back then. The devil promises that we'll gain worldly riches, applause, and approval if we follow his lead. Of course, this is done covertly and unconsciously. Few people willingly sell their souls to gain success. Yet, when we allow our ambitions to take precedence over our Bible study, church worship, and fellowship, the devil slowly wiggles his way into our lives.

Think of the rich young ruler who was unwilling to sacrifice his material wealth to follow Jesus (Mark 10:17–27). He gave up an opportunity to live and work with Jesus because financial security was more important to him! Jesus told us that no one can serve two masters, "for either he will hate the one and love the other, or he will be devoted to the one and despise the other. You cannot serve God and money" (Luke 16:13). Jesus taught us not to focus on acquiring earthly wealth, but to store up heavenly riches: "Do not lay up for yourselves treasures on earth, where moth and rust destroy and where thieves break in and steal, but lay up for yourselves treasures in heaven, where neither moth nor rust destroys and where thieves do not break in and steal" (Matthew 6:19–20). It would be a while before I'd understand the importance of Jesus' words.

I was using the formulas I'd learned in Christian Science, the New Age, and from years of studying Norman Vincent Peale to "manifest" my wants. I wasn't turning to God or asking for His guidance, because God seemed faraway. I thought of God as synonymous with "the universe," an impersonal but loving and wise energy force. How could you feel close to an energy force? That's why I'd turn instead to the angels, who seemed so friendly and accessible.

If you're ambitious, please be very careful! Test the spirits—and let your ambitions be purely about bringing glory to God and pleasing Him (Philippians 2:3).

I was seduced by the first-class lifestyle from my New Age teachings. Michael and I reclined in our first-class suite aboard an Emirates jet heading to Milan, Italy. It consisted of two reclining seats with ample legroom and amenities surrounded by a private wall within the commercial jet, like our own apartment. The Emirates first-class section was filled with these suites.

We were treated like rock stars on the New Age tours, mostly because ticket and book sales earned the producers *lots* of money. So, the producers made sure that Michael and I were comfortable in our travels. People are fond of demonizing the prosperity televangelists, but the same thing exists with the popular New Age teachers, all of whom are multimillionaires.

The fully reclining Emirates seats and the walls surrounding our suite allowed Michael and me to get some sleep as we flew to Milan. When we landed at European airports, we were usually met on the tarmac by a limo or private car. An airport official would board the jet and escort us down the steps into the waiting car. Then, while we relaxed in the airport lounge, someone retrieved our bags and processed our passports to enter the country. When we were in Switzerland, the airport lounge attendant brought us an assortment of full-sized Swiss lotions and toiletries as free gifts. We rarely stood in passport lines or at baggage carousels, and every whim was catered to, which eventually made us spoiled and entitled.

This was my proof that the New Age motto "follow your dreams" made sense. I didn't realize at the time that God's will is for us to follow Jesus, not ourselves. Back then, my focus was materialistic.

My spirituality was all about "manifesting" answers to my self-serving prayers for material things. Yet, even though I had everything material that you could want, I was still searching because material possessions cannot save or satisfy us. Only Jesus can.

One December when I arrived in Italy to give a workshop, my event producers surprised me with a fully decorated Christmas tree in my hotel room. Beneath the tree were dozens of wrapped presents, each containing Italian shoes and boots in my size. Another time we were whisked away to a seaside Italian villa, complete with cascading flowers on the patio trellis and a massage room next to the villa's kitchen. Our event producer arranged for Michael and me to have a couples massage right there in our room. Next we were treated to a viewing of the masterpiece mural *The Last Supper*, followed by a trip to Verona to see the tower credited to Romeo and Juliet.

While in Milan, we shopped at Cavalli and Etro and spent thousands on gowns that I wore onstage and in videos. This is one way that you can spot a false prophet, by the way. They often wear attention-grabbing designer clothing with loud prints or over-the-top expensive shoes. That's because false prophets want to glorify and call attention to themselves instead of to God, because of deep-seated insecurities related to the (sometimes unconscious) knowledge that they're sinning against God. You'll also hear false prophets boast and brag about how special they are instead of pointing people to the magnificence and glory of God. Jesus said, "The one who speaks on his own authority seeks his own glory; but the one who seeks the glory of him who sent him is true, and in him there is no falsehood" (John 7:18).

I'd often bring my friends with me on these trips, paying for all their expenses. We'd stay in penthouse suites in the finest hotels, dine on room service, ride in limousines, and indulge in high-adrenaline activities like scuba diving with sharks or swimming with manatees.

In each city I'd give workshops or speeches to groups of five hundred or more. The event producer would arrange for a limousine to drive us from our hotel to the venue, where we'd be escorted to a back-stage greenroom filled with yummy food and often a makeup artist.

The glamour of these all-expenses-paid, first-class speaking tours was also the experience Pastor Costi Hinn described having when he worked for his infamous prosperity preacher uncle, Benny Hinn. In his book, which I highly recommend, *God, Greed, and the (Prosperity) Gospel*, Costi Hinn wrote of the excess that came with his job: "I enjoyed more luxury than I ever could have imagined. It felt like I was hanging out with King Solomon. There are wealthy people who have lots of money but don't live lavishly; then there are wealthy people who have lots of money and know how to turn lavish novelty into normalcy. We were the latter."[1]

After Jesus opened Costi's eyes and he was saved, he went through a big culture shock, which I'd later experience, too, after salvation:

> I had gone from living in nearly ten thousand square feet to living in six hundred square feet. From driving a Hummer, to driving a Chrysler, to driving a Kia Soul, to riding my bike because my wife needed the car to go to work. . . . It wasn't glamorous, but it was honest. There were no luxuries, but there was no guilt either. People may have thought we had failed, but we felt we had hit the jackpot. I had peace. I could sleep at night. No one was being exploited because of my decisions.[2]

Sometime later, I'd personally experience what Costi had described—the peaceful elation of following Jesus instead of worldly success. I wish I could've discovered that truth much earlier in life, and I pray that someone reading this book will learn from my mistakes.

In the early years of my speaking tours, I'd personally walk through the audience and greet people before each workshop began. But as time went on, I found myself becoming increasingly paranoid of the public. I got it in my head that someone was going to kill me, so my publisher hired expensive security guards to walk and sit near me at my workshops. I was convinced that Christians were mad at me, so I thought they'd try to kill me while I was onstage.

That's the thing about the mindset of someone who's not obeying God: there's this sense that you're all alone in the world, and it's you against them. After Jesus saved me, I realized that I needn't fear death and that He is my refuge and my safety.

My very first workshops were small events held at Religious Science churches (a New Thought heretical religion related to Christian Science), and Mind-Body-Spirit conventions. I was a woman on a mission, so I traveled throughout North America and the United Kingdom giving workshops, often losing money after paying my own travel expenses. Back then, I was crammed into coach airline seats, riding in frightening taxi cabs, and staying in economy hotels.

Yet I was driven by an ambition that I now see was Satan masquerading as an angel of light (2 Corinthians 11:14). If you're ambitious, please pray carefully to determine your motives. I was fooled into believing that I was "saving the world" with my teachings. I encouraged my students to go save the world too. That's a common theme of demonic influence, this idea that you've been appointed to be a savior. Let us never forget that Jesus is the Savior of the world, not us. Let us always be humbled by God's absolute sovereignty. Only God could speak the universe into existence, not us. God doesn't need us to save the world. He doesn't need us to orchestrate His second coming. It's we who need to be saved by God.

In the early 1990s, I was approached by a group called "the Whole Life Expo," an organization that sponsored twice-monthly New Age conventions in various North American cities. A group of speakers and vendors traveled to each city's convention center. When the Whole Life Expo producers asked me, "Would you like to be a part of our traveling team of speakers?" I accepted without hesitation.

Finally, my travel expenses would be paid, and I'd even receive a small stipend for my efforts! Twice a month The Whole Life Expo set up in a convention center to offer lectures and products related to health and spirituality. Attendees paid a small entrance fee, but the bulk of the profits came from vendors paying for the right to have a booth at the convention.

As I walked along the convention hall with all the booths, the smell of incense permeated the air. Massage tables were filled with people receiving treatments, and women wearing long gowns gave tarot card readings on velvet-covered tables. Women holding brass finger cymbals and tie-dyed chiffon scarves danced in circles. Well-sculpted people demonstrated yoga poses. Stacks of New Age books and card decks for sale sat next to deity statues.

It all seemed so exotic and exciting! Plus, the New Age people seemed friendlier and more open-minded than anyone I'd previously met. They'd hug me, say I was a goddess, and exude a contagious enthusiasm. The part of me that had previously felt like an outcast as a child was nurtured by the sociability of New Agers. I was also hanging out at parties and backstage in greenrooms with famous New Age teachers, like Marianne Williamson, Wayne Dyer, Deepak Chopra, Louise Hay, James Redfield, and Neale Donald Walsch.

The Whole Life Expo conferences were held on Saturdays and Sundays. On Saturday evenings, the Expo organizers sponsored a party for all the speakers and vendors. We'd meet in the living room of a hotel suite where we were all staying, and there'd be food, wine, and beer. I noticed a lot of heavy drinking and people bringing different romantic partners each time. I decided that I'd never be like that, not realizing that I'd entered the devil's playground.

While the New Age promotes itself as the humble spiritual path, the truth is that big marketing underpins these expos. During my years touring as a New Age speaker, I was under tremendous pressure to promote events for ticket sales and to encourage participants to sign up for workshops and buy my books. The New Age dangles promises that you'll learn about your life purpose, find your soul mate, discover the secret to health and wealth, attain inner peace, and so on. All you need to do is buy this book and enroll in this workshop. After Jesus saved me, it was a huge relief to leave that pressure and those empty promises behind!

I've attended hundreds of New Age industry parties, and at each one the alcohol and hedonism flowed. Toward the end of the party, most people were drunk and flirting with one another. It's all about promoting yourself to become more famous and living your best life now, because the universalist and pluralistic beliefs say that everyone goes to heaven. Most New Agers also believe in reincarnation, and that you can do whatever you want without concern about the afterlife because you'll have other lives to "work out your karma," and eventually you and everyone else will end up in heaven.

The New Age also encourages you to "find your soul mate," which means an ideal, conflict-free relationship. According to New Age teachings, you'll instantly recognize and fall in love with your soul mate and enjoy a long-term happy relationship of seeing eye to eye on everything. If you're really fortunate, you'll have the ultimate spiritual relationship with your "twin flame," which is better than a soul mate. A twin flame is supposedly a person with whom you've lived and loved over several lifetimes of reincarnation.

These teachings result in New Age relationships breaking up the moment that conflict and differing opinions arise. You realize that your partner isn't identical to you, and so you leave that person to go find your *real* soul mate. The devil has set up this system so there's a revolving door of serial monogamy in the New Age. Long-term marriage is as rare in the New Age as it is in Hollywood. Broken and multiple successive marriages are the norm when you're continually seeking a conflict-free relationship instead of working on the marriage to which you've committed. One speaker I worked with seemed to bring a new woman to each event, and each time he'd introduce her as his wife. I lost count of how many wives of his I met.

Under this influence, I'm so ashamed now to admit that I also struggled through a few years of heavy wine drinking and relationship problems. Before my salvation, I didn't understand the solemn covenant of marriage, and I walked away when things got tough in search of my "true soul mate." In this quest, I remarried a nonbeliever who abused drugs. Without the solid foundation of Jesus at the center of our marriage, the union was doomed. I'd become exactly like the Whole Life Expo speakers I didn't want to be like. I was a wretched sinner, without realizing how the New Age teachings were eating away at my soul and wrecking my life.

About ten years before my salvation, I quit drinking because the constant hangovers were just too much. Then in 2009, at one of my New Age events, I met my husband, Michael, who was raised and baptized as a Methodist but had drifted away. We eventually married, and through the grace of God, we left the New Age together. Now Jesus, prayer, church, and Bible study are the center of our marriage. Finally, I have the love that I was always seeking! We have conflicts, but we work through them together. Now, thanks to Jesus, I am fully committed to being with my husband for the rest of my life, for better or worse.

After we were saved by Jesus, we realized that our prior divorces were sinful, and we repented. Michael and I were already married by the time we realized that our remarriage is biblically considered adulterous. Some people say that since our divorces occurred before our salvation, we will be forgiven. Other people have told us that Michael and I need to stay married, since divorcing to avoid adultery with a remarriage would incur additional sinfulness. We hold to the promise, "There is therefore now no condemnation for those who are in Christ Jesus" (Romans 8:1) and are thankful to Jesus for opening our eyes.

I wish I could rewind my life and be raised as a lifelong Christian who married another believer and had a committed, lifelong, Christ-centered marriage. But that's not how my life turned out. I was raised in a false religion and influenced by the devil and the false New Age teachings about finding your ideal soul mate. I've repented to God, deeply apologized to my children, and am very remorseful about my past. The best I can do now is to warn people to stay away from the New Age and to learn from my mistakes.

That hedonistic lifestyle of the New Age was a nonstop, adrenaline-filled adventure. I traveled the world with people I thought were friends, and we'd visit all the high-end designer stores in Milan, London, Paris, New York, Sydney, and Los Angeles, buying whatever we wanted. I didn't realize that I was spending money faster than I was earning it, and after taxes, I rarely had much money left over. That kept me in a cycle of continually giving workshops so that I'd have enough money to pay my bills. The devil is an evil genius, y'all. I grieve now thinking of how I could've helped impoverished families with that money!

When I first read the book of Ecclesiastes in the Bible, I could relate to Solomon's angst over the emptiness of materiality. In Ecclesiastes, we read how Solomon's pursuit of wealth, women, and experiences was motivated by pride, but ultimately led to humility as he realized it was all nothingness.

Pride had also motivated me to buy all those expensive gowns to wear on workshop stages. I cringed when I finally connected the dots between my childhood angst about being an out-of-style geek who was teased by the cool kids, and my overcompensation in adulthood to dress to the nines.

My pride stemmed from a sincere but misguided desire to be loved. Still, my sin of pride was that I was trying to glorify myself instead of giving glory to God. The New Age fans the flames of self-glory by encouraging everyone to use positive affirmations that we are wonderful, awesome, and amazing. While these affirmations temporarily boost confidence and mood, they're like eating sugar, which leads to a crash. The high is always followed by a low.

Pride is dangerous. Proverbs 16:18 teaches that pride leads to a fall and destruction. Indeed, pride led to the fallen angels (Isaiah 14:12–15).

In contrast, humility leads to God's favor and wisdom (Proverbs 3:34; 11:2). Pride is also associated with foolishness, while humility is linked with wisdom.

Author and pastor Burk Parsons said, "We are all prone to be puffed up with pride, so we have to pray against that every day. We have to flee from it, and run from it, because pride is one of the most pernicious sins that so easily creeps up within our souls, and it's there before we even know it."[3]

One of the many contrasts I notice now is that I'm more teachable. In fact, I'm *hungry* to learn about Scripture, so I love reading and studying the Bible. Before my salvation, I was accustomed to being the know-it-all expert. I was the prideful New Age teacher, and if someone tried to teach me anything, I became offended because I thought they were seeing me as inadequate.

Despite living in a fabulous palace and being the most famous king in the land, King Solomon wanted more. Toward the end of his life, Solomon tragically allowed his pagan wives to build idolatrous altars at the temple. Even more tragically, Solomon joined his wives in worshiping pagan deities. This resulted in God's judgment against Israel, the nation being divided, and eventually exile and destruction (1 Kings 11:1–13).

In Ecclesiastes, Solomon teaches that everything in this world is utterly temporary, based on the Hebrew word *hevel*. English translations render this word as "transient," "vanity," or "meaningless," with the same point that riches, relationships, and achievements aren't fulfilling. Instead of chasing after the world's temptations, we should embrace wisdom and avoid foolishness so we can be bold, joyful, and reverent while there is still time (1:12–2:26; 4:1–16; 5:10–6:9; 9:13–10:20; 11:1–10).[4]

These themes of Ecclesiastes are timeless issues that are applicable today for people dealing with existential issues of meaning and purpose in life. We can save ourselves time, trouble, and money if we allow

Solomon's hard-won lessons to sink in: that this world offers nothing of lasting value.

The devil only offers empty promises that you'll gain love and happiness if you follow his lead. Now, very few people would consciously follow the devil. However, the devil disguises himself in evil-genius ways. One of these ways is by telling you to follow your heart and your dreams. *Go ahead. You've had a hard life. You deserve the best!* he'll say through the world's messages. And it's so easy to agree with these seemingly logical and innocent encouragements.

That's why we must continually remember:

> *"Whatever you do, do it all for the glory of God."*
> —1 CORINTHIANS 10:31 (NLT)

The Holy Spirit will convict us when we veer into self-glory, but of course we can try to ignore Him. Some good questions to ask and pray about before making decisions are:

- Does this glorify God?
- In what way does this glorify God?
- Am I trying to make myself appear special with this decision?
- Am I trying to fill my hunger for God's love by seeking the approval of people instead?
- Am I willing to completely lean on and trust God with all my heart, even if it means going in a different direction?

Praying on these kinds of questions helps us stay honest with the Holy Spirit and keeps our hearts teachable. We are the clay and He is the potter (Isaiah 64:8).

FIVE

False Prophecy

Before I was saved, I traveled around the world for twenty-two years, giving workshops. It seemed that with each passing year, I grew increasingly paranoid about someone physically harming me at one of my workshops. I was teaching about peace but living in fear. How hypocritical, yet I wasn't aware of this condition at the time. I became more aloof in public. I made sure to have convention center security guards with me at all times. It's ironic that I used to teach about angels, particularly the archangel Michael, providing protection. But I must not have really believed that, looking back on my actions.

My workshops consisted of me giving a general overview of angels from a New Age perspective, which means I taught heresy. Five minutes into the start of each workshop, I'd invariably see two or more conservatively dressed women get up and leave. Looking back, they were probably Christians who thought I'd be giving a biblically based seminar about God's angels. At that time though, I thought that angels were wish granters who would help you get everything from a good parking place to your soul mate husband or a successful business. At each seminar I'd also give what I called "angel readings," which are basically psychic readings purportedly with the information coming from the person's guardian angels or from an archangel.

A little warning, because for the next little while, my story is going to get even weirder. Looking back now as a born-again Christian, I can barely recognize myself in these situations. Yet they are part of my testimony, and for those who are currently in deception—or who have loved ones in deception—the following information is important to know. I'm relaying all of this so that you'll have insights into the underbelly of false prophecy.

It began in childhood, and please keep in mind that I was raised in a false religion. I had terrible nightmares about an elderly man taking me to see other planets and showing me the future of earth. I also had waking visions of ghoulish people peering into my bedroom window. When I cried to my parents, they decided I was seeing reflections from the family television set, even though it was way down the hall from my bedroom. I learned to keep my visions to myself, because when I'd tell the neighborhood kids, "Look over there! Who's that man hiding in the bushes?" the other kids would shrug their shoulders and claim they couldn't see anyone.

I soon developed a reputation as the weird kid of the neighborhood, and I was frequently shunned by others. I sat alone in my bedroom a lot, heavy with loneliness and feeling misunderstood. That's when I'd see floating colored lights swirling around my bedroom, halfway between my bed and the ceiling. They were accompanied by an otherworldly whirring sound, like some cosmic gears grinding with squeaky parts. It sounds terrifying, doesn't it? Yet I found it comforting, because "someone" cared about me enough to visit. I didn't know who or what these dancing lights were, but I later believed they were angels who'd come to comfort a lonely child.

As I mentioned before, I did have two close friends in adolescence who are still good friends today, Anita and Silvia. Beyond them, though, I was an off-putting oddball without many friends. When boys paid attention to me in high school, I misread their signals. I thought they wanted to be friends. My social interactions were awkward and painful.

Most people who become psychotherapists do so with the intention of understanding themselves. That was true for me when I majored in psychology in college. After the birth of my two sons, Charles and Grant, I continued attending college part-time and eventually earned a BA and an MA in counseling psychology from Chapman University in Orange, California.

I mentioned earlier that I worked for a psychiatric clinic in Lancaster, California, where I had an outpatient practice devoted to treating eating disorders. Most of my clients were sweet middle-aged women struggling with obesity, and I'd occasionally see some women with anorexia and bulimia issues. I'd taken extra classes in the treatment of eating disorders and had previously worked at the inpatient unit for alcohol and drug abuse treatment, plus had been an administrator and therapist at an outpatient adolescent treatment center. I was well versed in counseling those with addictions and eating disorders.

Yet, something started to happen as I'd sit with my clients. For the first time since childhood, I began having visions again. Usually, the vision would be like this:

Me: "How was your week, Sally?"
Sally: "Oh, I did my best to not overeat."

Then I'd suddenly see a vision of Sally overeating at the local ice cream shop. I could even see the flavors she'd eaten! So I'd casually ask if she'd stopped in the ice cream shop, and Sally would cry and admit that she'd been binge eating. These spontaneous visions happened a lot with my clients! It was as if I was seeing movies in my mind of what that person did. I rationalized that the information was helpful to their treatment, and since I'd had visions in childhood, I dismissed these experiences as normal and positive.

Of course, I didn't reveal to my clients that I was having visions. They just thought I was a really good therapist. Soon my private practice was filled with clients referring their friends to see me. The results of my unspoken visions led to worldly success at my clinic.

The visions continued, even though I wasn't invoking them or praying for my clients. The thing is, these visions were detailed, accurate, and helpful. So why would I suspect that they could originate from a malevolent source?

The enemy mixes truth and comfort into his lies so that we'll naively trust and follow his messages. He also works undercover, pretending to be our own thoughts. *The Screwtape Letters* by C. S. Lewis is a good book to read to learn more about this tactic. The enemy even masquerades as an angel (2 Corinthians 11:14). Some people mistakenly believe they are hearing from God or the Holy Spirit when it's really the enemy with his seemingly "accurate messages" that contain Trojan horse hidden lies.

The enemy's messages derailed and deceived me for decades. For example, I had a long-distance client I counseled on the telephone about her eating disorders. One day during our phone session, I had a thought: *Ask her what her guardian angel would say about this situation.* Now, I hadn't shared my visions or beliefs with any of my clients. So I kind of argued with this thought, saying that I couldn't possibly veer the conversation in a weird spiritual direction.

The thought persisted, though. I took a deep breath and asked my client, "What do you think your guardian angel would say about this situation?" My client was silent as I mentally kicked myself for my unprofessionalism. Then she quietly said, "I'm not sure what my guardian angel would say."

My thoughts prompted me to encourage my client to ask her guardian angel for a message, which I did. After a few moments, my client shyly answered what she believed her guardian angel was saying. I watched the whole scenario like an outside observer, and especially noticed that my client found the "message" she received as helpful. A month later, she reported putting this message into action, with amazing results of a healing and a job promotion. We were both convinced that this message must've been from her guardian angel.

Now, I wasn't raised with a strong sense of angels. The Christian Science Church mentions them but doesn't have a theology about angels. I also hadn't read much of the Bible, so I didn't realize the biblical view of angels was that only God sends messengers. We humans don't ask for angels, nor do we ask for angelic messages or favors. The reason? God is protecting us from demons posing as angels.

Just as I had my own version of Jesus, so, too, did I base my belief about angels on my personal experiences. It was such a lovely belief too! How nice to believe that we each have loving guardians hovering nearby, awaiting our prayers, whims, and wishes. That's a nice belief, except it's not true. What's true is that many people believe this, and the belief makes people vulnerable to the enemy taking advantage of us.

The Bible is filled with angel stories, yet not one of these stories involves a human calling on an angel or *seeking* a message from an angel. I've searched from Genesis 1 to Revelation 22, and there is no biblical basis for the action of asking for an angel message. Psalm 91 seems to suggest that we all have guardian angels, and Psalm 34:7 says the angel of the Lord encamps around everyone who fears God. But the term *guardian angel* doesn't appear in the Bible.

The belief that we can call on archangel Michael for protection is also unbiblical. I had also fallen for that belief, and unfortunately, I taught the belief to others in my books and workshops. *What's the harm in that?* someone may ask. Well, we're repeatedly told throughout the Bible to turn only to God for help and direction. The archangel Michael shows up in the Bible for specific purposes, but not to provide individual protection for humans.

In the book of Daniel, the angel Gabriel and the archangel Michael appear together to the prophet (Daniel 8–10). Gabriel explains that Daniel's vision is of the end times (8:15–17), and Michael assists in the spiritual warfare against the prince of Persia (10:13). Biblical scholar Dr. Michael Heiser, author of *Angels*, has developed a deeper understanding about Michael and the angel of the Lord by studying the original Hebrew writings in the Old Testament. Heiser has written that Michael and Gabriel are the lone angels mentioned by name in the Bible, and only Michael is called an archangel in the New Testament (Jude 9).[1]

In my New Age days, my beliefs about angels were an amalgamation of my experiences during my sessions with clients, thoughts I'd have during meditation, and reading New Age books on angels, including the angel dictionaries. I also incorporated Catholic and Eastern Orthodox traditions about archangels and blended that with the biblical annunciation passages. In other words, my angel beliefs and teachings were all over the place. I deeply regret that I didn't first study the entire Bible to gain a solid understanding about angels and archangels.

After the "success" with my client who had seemed to get a message from her guardian angel, I was encouraged to try this method with more of my eating-disordered clients. We had similar positive results, so I kept going. My private practice was becoming increasingly booked up, and I was concerned whether I could help everyone who was requesting appointments.

I went for a walk and prayed for God to reveal what I should do next. I still thought of God as a universal energy of love and wisdom. I didn't have a personal relationship with God; after all, I was an unrepentant sinner at that time. I also wasn't reading my Bible, which is the primary way that God speaks to us. When we ask for a spiritual message without discernment, as I was at that moment, we are vulnerable for the enemy to intervene. The enemy pretends that he's God, Jesus, the Holy Spirit, an angel, or whomever we're seeking. Remember that Jesus Himself called the devil "the father of lies" (John 8:44). The enemy's guidance is cloaked in the illusion that you're doing something unselfish and helping to save the world. And that's exactly what kind of guidance I received that day.

The guidance was for me to hold classes teaching others how to receive messages from their guardian angels. I was "told" in this guidance, which came through my thoughts, that people would know they were personally selected to take this class. They would be given the time, money, transportation, and babysitting to attend this class. Now, doesn't that sound like a neat and tidy package? I thought it was from God, but why would God ask me to sin against Him? I didn't realize it at the time, but I was about to start a "false prophecy school" that would run internationally for two decades.

In these classes, I taught students to ask their guardian angels for messages and then sit quietly while they noticed the first thought that popped into their heads or hearts. I also encouraged them to each sit across from another class member while holding hands, and silently ask for guardian angel messages about the other person.

The accuracy of these messages was mind-blowing! We'd all receive specific details about our classmates' lives that we couldn't have previously known. Things like their mothers' names, childhood incidents, and the health histories of people who were strangers to us before the class began. We were all impressed that because the messages were accurate and comforting, they must be from angels. None of us worried that these "angels" could be undercover demons. Such thoughts would be considered negative.

We weren't doing mind reading or noticing body language. There were no parlor tricks involved. We simply asked for guardian angel messages, then noticed what popped into our heads or hearts. We even said "prayers of protection" to ensure that the messages really were from guardian angels. So, what's the problem? Well, God doesn't provide protection so that we can sin against Him by seeking counseling from demons-in-disguise. And these "accurate and comforting messages" also contained guidance that began to slowly pull the students away from the Bible, Jesus, the church, Christian family members, and their relationship with God.

Each class was filled with people who identified as "former Christians" and "recovering Catholics," a term frequently used by ex-Catholics who say they were traumatized by Catholic priests or services. Class members usually wore cross necklaces and said they were raised in a Christian faith. But they'd drifted away, blaming hypocrisy and abuse in the church as the primary reason. Most said they had doubts about the authenticity of the Bible, and they held universalist beliefs that Jesus loved and accepted everyone, regardless of that person's actions. Calling out someone's sins wasn't loving, according to this worldview.

I taught this class from the 1990s through the 2010s in the United States, the United Kingdom, Europe, and Australia. I also gave keynote speeches about angels in even larger geographical areas. At my angel speeches, I'd demonstrate angel readings by doing cold readings on audience members from the stage. By this point, each audience was filled with from five hundred to four thousand people, so with stage lights all I could see were darkened figures in the chairs.

I prayed to receive messages for audience members, and I'd frequently hear or think of a name, including the way it was spelled. "Is there a Stefani, spelled with an *f*, in the audience tonight? Your guardian angel has a message for you." And up would pop two or three audience members named Stefani. Then I would "tune in" to my body to get a sense of *which* Stefani was getting the message. Usually I'd feel a pull in a specific direction of the audience. I couldn't actually see most of the audience members clearly from the stage.

After narrowing it down to one Stefani (or whichever name popped up at that time), I "tuned in" to whatever thoughts popped into my head or heart. Sometimes I'd also see a vision of an angel floating above the person's shoulder. Or I'd see an image or have a gut feeling about a deceased person or pet (which is mediumship, something that God clearly forbids, but I didn't know that at the time). A few times I even saw beings who looked like the old-fashioned paintings of Jesus. Had I read 1 John 4 and tested the spirits, I would've realized they were demons trying to lead me away from the real Jesus and the Bible.

I learned to be unfiltered during these angel reading demonstrations. I'd say whatever popped into my head or heart. Sometimes I'd hesitate and rationalize that the message couldn't possibly be true. For example, I had the thought that a young woman in the audience had lost her mother. But I hesitated saying anything, thinking, *She's too young to have lost her mother! What if I'm wrong and I offend or worry her?* At that point the young woman told me that she'd recently lost her mother. I mentally hit my head and thought, *Duh! I knew that! Why did I hesitate in saying it?* After a while, I stopped second-guessing myself and would just spit out everything I saw, thought, felt, or heard during these sessions.

Every time, the messages were gentle, sweet, compassionate, loving, comforting . . . and accurate! I'd receive messages about people's future, and they'd confirm the accuracy months later. I'd get messages about a person's ideal career occupation, what's called "life purpose" in the New Age, and the person would say that was his or her hobby and dream job.

My point is that I had no reason to doubt that these messages were from God. The demand for me to give angel readings and teach others how to give angel readings was immense. My classes and speeches were sold out everywhere.

In the spirit of transparency, I also want to admit right here that there were times when I was onstage and feeling tired, unwell, or uninspired. So, I'd revert to a few "stage gimmicks," because I didn't know what else to do and everyone was staring at me and had bought tickets to hear me give readings. I'm telling you about this because you'll see other false prophets do this.

The gimmick would be for me to say I was getting a message that someone in the audience had shoulder pain or upper back pain. Of course someone did, as it's a pervasive condition, and I knew that. So I would narrow it down to someone near the front of the audience so that everyone could see what was going to happen. Next, I would say that there was someone in the audience who had healing hands or a spiritual gift of healing. Many people would raise their hands. Then I would ask one of those "healers" to go over to the person with the back pain and put their hands on the place that was sore. I would continue with my workshop and keep checking back in with the healer and the person in need to ask how they were doing. There would always be a positive response of warm feelings, reduction of pain, and so forth.

I knew this message about "someone has back pain in the audience" was conjured by me, to keep the workshop going. But I rationalized that we had a real healing effect, so the ends justified the means.

Similarly, when I wasn't inspired onstage, I'd sometimes revert to saying, "There's someone in this audience who is guided to write a book but is intimidated by the process." Several hands would shoot up, and I'd select one person to chat with. Because I'd taught "How to become a published writer" courses through the years, I was able to give practical, real-world advice. But the genesis of the conversation was based on disingenuousness, for which I'm sorry. I've especially repented about this because one person in my audience, whom I encouraged to write, ended up becoming a popular writer of heretical books, and he credits that audience "reading" I gave him as motivating him to write.

I'm ashamed of this dishonesty now, and I've repented of it. I apologize to you if you were in my audience. One of the ways you can spot a false prophet is by seeing him repeat the same gimmick from workshop to workshop, like I did. For example, I've noticed that a high percentage of false prophets tell the person they're giving a reading to, "You were made for such a time as this," quoting Esther 4:14 in a way that seems to tickle people's itching ears (2 Timothy 4:3). I used to give false hope like that, too, because I gave people what they wanted to hear to please them in that moment.

Pastor Chris Rosebrough of the Fighting for the Faith YouTube channel, which I highly recommend, recently asked me how I could lie to people onstage that I was "getting messages" when these were just gimmicks. Pastor Rosebrough said that he'd noticed false prophets doing repetitive gimmicks and lying that they were getting genuine messages from God in the process.

I answered Pastor Rosebrough that I was now ashamed that I'd broken God's ninth commandment about lying, but at the time my conscience was seared (1 Timothy 4:2), so I rarely noticed the Holy Spirit's convictions. Plus, I was unsaved, so the Holy Spirit didn't dwell within me. I believe that God was judging my rebelliousness by allowing me to sin. I've now repented of this sin and continue to do so.

Besides these gimmicks, though, the majority of my "readings" were genuine from the standpoint of me passively receiving information that I couldn't have known beforehand. Through hundreds, perhaps thousands, of readings during those twenty-two years I was onstage, on radio, and on television, I was amazed at what came through. I'd receive names, places, dates, and other specifics on behalf of the person I was reading. These impressions would come as a combination of visions (inside and outside my mind), words that I'd hear, feelings, and thoughts. The fact that people would validate the accuracy of my readings encouraged me to keep going. I had no idea that I was receiving this information from demons masquerading as angels!

Since becoming a Christian, I've received lots of letters from people who want to know how psychics, mediums, channelers, angel readers, and prophets could possibly be fake or frauds if their information is both accurate and comforting. The answer is that Satan knows how to hook us in. As nonphysical beings, demons have the ability to know our past and present and to predict our likely future. Only God is omniscient (all knowing). However, the devil carefully studies human behavior and also influences our actions unless we're vigilantly guarded. Demons also know how to package their messages in a super-sweet way that appears to be loving and kind.

The demons feed true information in a comforting way through psychics, mediums, channelers, angel readers, and prophets. But then they mix in messages designed to lead you away from church, the Bible, and the true saving grace of Jesus. The demons want to addict us to the psychics so we will stop leaning on God and the Bible for guidance. Always remember that Satan is a smooth-talking and charming liar. He's the ultimate narcissistic sociopath. Jesus said that Satan is the father of lies (John 8:44).

Some people try to convince me that it's okay to mix in a little bit of New Age with their Christianity. "So what if I read my horoscope or go to yoga?" they ask me. "God knows my heart." Jesus also warned us about hypocrisy, such as claiming to be Christ-followers, while consciously following the world's ways. It's hypocrisy to say that we trust God, while simultaneously consulting our horoscopes or a psychic to peek into the future. It's hypocrisy to say that Jesus gives us peace, while also insisting that we need alcohol, yoga, or Eastern meditation to have peace.

Jesus' words are alarmingly convicting: "Beware of the leaven of the Pharisees, which is hypocrisy. Nothing is covered up that will not be revealed, or hidden that will not be known. Therefore whatever you have said in the dark shall be heard in the light, and what you have whispered in private rooms shall be proclaimed on the housetops" (Luke 12:1–3). In other words, God sees everything we think and do, so if we believe that, our lives will reflect it. Again, it's not that we're saved by our obedience, but because we are saved, we want to obey. Our obedience is a fruit of our salvation.

Horoscopes and astrology are forbidden pagan practices because God wants us to lean on Him for answers (Deuteronomy 4:19; Isaiah 47:13–15). In Romans 1, the apostle Paul warns against worshiping the creation (such as stars and planets) instead of the Creator. Why turn to the stars for answers, when you can go directly to the One who made the stars?

We are exhorted to glorify God in everything we do (1 Corinthians 10:31). Astrology doesn't glorify God, and neither does yoga. The meaning of the word *yoga* is "yoked"or "union," specifically a yoked union to the Hindu creator deity. Each of the yoga poses is designed to worship a specific Hindu deity.[2] Does that glorify our one true God? No, it certainly does not. God said that He won't share glory with pagan deities (Isaiah 42:8).

What if you listen to Bible verses while doing yoga? Doesn't that undo the pagan basis of yoga? Well, think about this question: Would saying Bible verses while practicing tarot card readings, astrology, mediumship, or other forbidden practices "undo" their pagan origins? Certainly not!

The term "holy yoga" is an oxymoron, because the two words cancel out each other. The primary reason to avoid yoga in any form is because we love God and want to obey and glorify Him. Another important reason is that engaging in pagan practices like yoga can open you up to demonic influence and lead you astray from the gospel.

What about basic stretching? Yes, of course, it's a good idea to stretch your muscles. For example, stretch in bed before getting up. Or, lay a towel on the floor and stretch your arms and legs. Curl up in a ball. Do lunges. Just don't do any yoga moves, which aren't natural movements anyway.

I was traveling to give workshops nonstop while constantly writing books and appearing on television and radio. For two decades, I rarely unpacked the essential basics from my suitcase. I'd come home as a pit stop to get clean clothing and have my hair done.

What I deeply regret is that I only saw my sons if I took them on the road with me, which I frequently did. After a while, my son Charles, who seemed to have a natural gift for receiving angel messages, would appear onstage with me. My younger son, Grant, helped me behind the scenes with engineering and playing music for my podcasts and building and managing my websites. Charles, Grant, and I would travel to cities where I'd give workshops, and they would man the table where my books or event tickets were sold. I also took my sons with me to the television and radio stations where I was interviewed, and they often appeared on programs with me.

My biggest regret is inculcating my sons into the New Age deception teachings. Sadly, I'd also talk with New Age audience members about how to deal with their Christian family members who were upset that they were attending my workshops. I tried to offer loving support and advice, but I definitely wasn't advocating anything biblical at that time. Now I apologize and say to them, "Your family was correct after all! None of us should have attended that demon-infested New Age workshop!"

I sincerely believe that God is sovereign over all things, and as Romans 8:28 and Genesis 50:20 teach, God can use all things for good. As the late R. C. Sproul wrote, "It's not that evil is good, but that God allows evil to use for his good purpose."[3] Maybe someday I'll mature in my faith enough to live regret-free. I realize that's part of trusting God and taking responsibility for my choices. But I'd be dishonest if I said that I am regret-free. One of my biggest regrets was missing the intersection set before me in the early 1990s.

At that time, my family and I lived on the Balboa peninsula of

Newport Beach, California, and the local United Methodist Christ Church by the Sea offered evening Bible study classes. I was drawn to this class, so my sons and I started attending weekly. The pastor was warm and gave lessons on beginning principles of Bible study, which my young sons and I appreciated because we were beginners. We began attending church services on Sundays, and soon the ladies invited me to their gatherings.

But I was confused, undiscerning, and spiritually blind, because I didn't know the difference between what was being taught at the Methodist church and what I'd learned in the Christian Science church in my younger years. It sounds so crazy, but I believed that *all* Christian churches were basically alike. Some seemed more open-minded to me, but I thought they were essentially the same. In addition to attending the Methodist church, my sons and I also went to the local Unity and Religious Science churches. I was hungry for God's truth but confused about how to find it.

I'd also listen to the local Calvary Chapel church's radio program every time I drove my car. The Calvary Chapel headquarters was close to my home, and I loved listening to their programs. I even called in to the radio show with my questions about Christianity, such as, "What does it mean to fear God?" The hosts were always nice to me, and one time when I quoted Norman Vincent Peale on the air, they gently corrected me that Peale was not Christian.

Yet, instead of continuing with the Methodist Bible studies, or attending Calvary Chapel, I dove into Religious Science, which is related to Christian Science. Ernest Holmes, the founder of Religious Science, was a student of the mesmerizer (hypnotist) Phineas Quimby, along with Mary Baker Eddy (founder of Christian Science), and the Fillmores (founders of Unity Church).

Quimby taught that experience and personal revelation were more authoritative than the Bible. This led to Mary Baker Eddy saying the Bible is no more important than a history book, and the Fillmores and Holmeses saying that the Bible was equal to all the holy books of all religions. Mary Baker Eddy said that her "divinely inspired" book, *Science and Health*, not the Bible, contained the "absolute truth."[4] We must beware of people who claim to have a higher truth than the Bible.

SIX

Apostasy, Heresy, and Confusion

Just as all Scripture is God-breathed and internally consistent, so are all false teachings devil-breathed, and that's why they are uniform and consistent. When I hear or read messages from false prophets, they sound exactly like my old days.

The apostle John told us to "test the spirits," to know whether they're from God or the devil, which are the only two possibilities (1 John 4:1). John gave us the test to know if a spirit is from God, such as a true angel or the Holy Spirit:

> By this you know the Spirit of God: every spirit that confesses that Jesus Christ has come in the flesh is from God, and every spirit that does not confess Jesus is not from God. This is the spirit of the antichrist, which you heard was coming and now is in the world already. (1 John 4:2–3)

John's warning is vital for all Christians to tuck into our hearts, because false prophets teach a false view of Jesus. In the New Age, false prophets teach that Jesus is "an ascended master" who was a mortal man and who is buddies with deities from other religions, such as Hinduism and Buddhism. In the New Age, it's considered "hate speech" if you don't say that all religions lead to God.

Testing the spirits means analyzing the "prophetic message" to see whether it confesses who Jesus really is: fully God and fully man who came to earth to take the punishment we deserve for our sins. If the "prophetic message," like the ones I used to deliver, teaches a false view of Jesus—that He was "just a man" or that "He emptied His divinity while on earth" or that "He's an ascended master"—you can be certain that it's a demon masquerading as an angel or pretending to be the Holy Spirit.

Test everything by asking:

- Does this message lead me toward Jesus or away from Jesus?
- Does this message encourage me to study the Bible, or does the spirit imply that we can follow its messages instead of the Bible?
- Does this message bring glory to God, or is it encouraging me to glorify myself or the false prophet?
- Does this message contradict what the Bible says?

I believe that false prophets are usually unaware that they're being used by demons to deliver messages that contradict the Bible, discourage Bible study, and lead people away from the true Jesus. Most heresies deny that Jesus was fully God and fully human during His earthly ministry. These are the most common heresies that false prophets present:

- **Adoptionism** teaches that Jesus is the Son of God because God adopted Him as His father. Many teachers of adoptionism say that Jesus was adopted at the moment of His baptism.[1]

- **Arianism** is the heresy that denies the full divinity of Jesus and says that Jesus was a human created by God and sent to earth by God to be a good example for humanity.
- **Docetism** denies the humanity of Jesus during His earthly ministry, and was the heresy popularized by the Gnostics that Jesus was a spirit who only appeared to be human.
- **Dominionism** denies the biblical gospel of salvation, which is by faith in Jesus Christ and His shed blood on the cross, and instead teaches that mankind is responsible for salvation by setting up a "kingdom of God" as a literal and physical kingdom to be "advanced" on Earth. In complete contradiction to the Bible, Dominionism says that Jesus cannot or will not return until the church has taken dominion by gaining control of the earth's governmental and social institutions.[2]
- **Kenosis** or **kenoticism** says that Jesus was fully God before He came to earth, but that He emptied His divinity and so was only human during His earthly ministry.
- **Modalism** denies that the Holy Trinity consists of three separate persons: the Father, the Son, and the Holy Spirit, and claims that God is one person who can take on three distinct forms.

Please familiarize yourself with these and other heresies, to safeguard yourself against deceptive teaching. Remember: just because a person is called a pastor or a modern-day apostle or modern-day prophet, and just because a person is famous and has popular books and videos, and just because a person is onstage, with lots of cheering audience members, and just because a person is holding a Bible and quoting Scripture—he or she still could be teaching deceptively.

As the late theologian R. C. Sproul wrote about Jesus' nature during His incarnation, "The divine nature of Christ during the incarnation was fully divine. Christ did not give up any divinity when He took on Himself a human nature. All the divine attributes are retained in the person of Christ. And when the divine nature adds a human nature, the human nature does not lack any of its humanity. Christ's human nature is fully human."[3]

When I look back on my life as a false prophet, I'm ashamed and amazed at how completely blind I was to the gospel truth! I remember being invited by New Age event producers to give an evening talk at the St. James Church, in Piccadilly, London. It was a beautiful historic church rented for New Age evening events. I was at the height of my deception as I opened that evening's talk by saying how wonderful that it was "Wesak," which is the day credited as Buddha's birthday. I then discussed the current astrological configurations.

Back then, I thought that "the more friends we have in heaven, the better." I deeply regret this belief and teaching now, of course. At that time, I sincerely believed that we could call on and receive equal help from all the religious deities, plus our deceased loved ones. Like a lot of false prophets, I taught about Jesus plus others. I didn't understand and probably wouldn't have believed back then John 14:6: "Jesus said to him, 'I am the way, and the truth, and the life. No one comes to the Father except through me.'"

New Agers also hold to beliefs in universalism and pluralism. Let's look at these terms and beliefs with the help of Dr. Todd Miles, author of *A God of Many Understandings*:

- **Universalism:** The hope that in the end, everyone will be reconciled to God. Universalism can be pluralistic (the belief that all paths lead to God) or inclusivist (the belief that God will eventually save everyone).
- **Pluralism:** When people say "universalism," they often are really referring to pluralism, which is the belief that every path and every religion leads to God. To the pluralist, Christ's life and death on the cross are powerful examples of a life committed to

God. The pluralist says that you don't have to believe in, have faith in, or follow Jesus to come to God.[4]

Dr. Miles wrote:

In its most basic form, the assertion of pluralism is that there are many paths to God. According to Christian Scriptures, the response to that pluralist assertion is: there are many paths to many gods, but only one path to the living God. . . . The Lord's response to those who worship other gods is critical . . . He forbids the worship of other gods. . . . The Bible is also clear that although there are many paths to many gods, there is only one path to the supreme God.[5]

Universalism and pluralism hold that everyone's going to heaven no matter what. If pushed, most universalists and pluralists will admit they don't believe Hitler or similar evildoers are in heaven. They will then amend their philosophy to say that "all *good* people go to heaven."

That's when we can take a page from the evangelist Ray Comfort of Living Waters Ministries, who asks unsaved people, "Do you think you're a good person?" Most people answer, "Yes, of course!" Then, with his disarmingly charming New Zealand accent, Ray asks, "Have you ever stolen anything, including candy when you were a child?" Most people will answer yes, they have. Ray next asks, "How many lies do you think you've told in your life?" People stammer that they can't count how many.

In his excellent book *Banana Man: The True Story of How a Demeaning Nickname Opened Amazing Doors for the Gospel*, Ray Comfort wrote, "Remember that the preaching of the cross is foolishness to those who are perishing (see 1 Corinthians 1:18). Instead of hearing the gospel, mockers need to hear the Law. When Paul spoke of 'warning every man' he was clearly referring to the Law, not the gospel. The word 'gospel' means 'good news,' and good news is not a warning." Ray said that we should witness to unrepentant sinners about the serious consequences of sin and teach about the Moral Law (the Ten Commandments) that we are all still under today.[6] By the way, I highly recommend watching Ray Comfort's "Living Waters" evangelism videos on YouTube for great examples of witnessing to unbelievers. Perhaps if Ray Comfort or someone using his style of evangelizing had approached me during my apostate years, I could have converted earlier.

At the time of my Piccadilly church talk, though, I still held my erroneous "the more friends in heaven, the better" pluralistic beliefs. About thirty minutes into the talk, a man in the audience raised his hand. When I asked the mic runner, the person walking around the event with a handheld cordless microphone, to please go to the man so we could all hear his question, I was surprised when the man angrily confronted me. "Why haven't you mentioned God or Jesus even once so far?" he growled loudly at me, which fit into my stereotype that Christians were angry people.

I said to him gently in front of everyone, "You seem to be angry. What's going on that's making you so angry?" The man got quiet, and I assumed he backed down because I'd responded with gentleness. Now I realize that he had "righteous anger"—anger over someone dishonoring God—that my talk in a Christian church was unbiblical. I wasn't honoring God with my talk. I was pouring out New Age nonsense that came from my deceived worldview. That's how spiritually blind I was back then; false prophets are blind to the gospel truth.

"How can I witness to my loved one who's in the New Age?" is a question I now receive daily. I'm not sure if anyone could have reached me back then. The devil essentially puts blinders around people's spiritual eyes, ears, and hearts and then fills them with a worldview that's the opposite of Christianity. Just as he did with Eve in the garden, the devil introduces doubts about God's Word: "Oh, God didn't really mean that!" (Genesis 3:1–5). The devil whispers into our minds that the Bible is a myth or that it has been tampered with. He convinces people that the Roman Catholic Church and the government have orchestrated Christianity to manipulate the population. He tells you that you're "woke" if you realize "the truth" that God is simply the "universe" who responds to your positive thoughts. And I'm ashamed to say that I fell for those lies before Jesus saved me.

So, if your loved ones are tangled in New Age deception, do your best to share the gospel with them. Talk with them about the Ten Commandments, and take them through the "Are You a Good Person?" test from Ray Comfort's LivingWaters.com website.[7] Don't be surprised or take it personally if your loved ones become offended by your evangelizing. After all, the worldly belief is that we're all good people, we're all going to heaven, and we don't need a savior to get there. As Ray told me during our interview, "The gospel is inherently offensive to most people."[8] Nonetheless, we sometimes *need* to be offended by the gospel to realize that we are sinners and we need Jesus as our Lord and Savior.

During that time of apostasy and confusion, I wrote books and magazine articles related to my psychology work. One of my books attracted the attention of the producers of the television show *The 700 Club*, who asked me to appear on their Valentine's Day show. They first asked, "Are you a Christian?" to which I wholeheartedly answered, "Yes." I wasn't trying to fool them. I honestly believed I was a Christian.

The 700 Club flew me to their city-within-a-city in Virginia. It's the most amazing place, complete with everything you'd need inside of a walled-in location. They put me up at the hotel within their campus, where I read the copy of Pat Robertson's biography that came with the room. The next morning, we all met in the greenroom backstage to hold hands in a circle and pray before going on the air. For some reason, they asked me to say the prayer. I wasn't shy about praying—I'd been praying my whole life. I just didn't realize that my theology was under the influence of false teachings. Nonetheless, I said a prayer from my heart, to which someone commented, "That's one of my favorite Bible passages." All was well, and I went on the show and talked about romance and Valentine's Day.

After the show wrapped that day, we all went to a restaurant on the campus to enjoy lunch. There were about twenty-five of us sitting around the large oblong table. Someone suggested that we go around the table, introducing ourselves and saying the denomination of the church we attended, starting on the other side of the table from me. One by one, people said they were Baptists, Presbyterians, Lutherans, and so forth. When it was my turn, I could have said truthfully that I attended the Methodist church, because I still did on occasion. But it felt more honest to say that I attended the Religious Science church, because I more frequently attended there. As soon as I said the words "Religious Science," the words became frosty and hung above the table. People cleared their throats and fidgeted, and lunch was hurriedly finished. I was aware of the uncomfortable silence, but I didn't realize it had anything to do with my answer. That's how deceived I was!

A *700 Club* staff member escorted me to my hotel room to gather my belongings. As I closed my suitcase, she gently asked me, "Aren't you afraid that God's mad at you for attending the Religious Science church?" Her question stunned me, because I'd never before thought of God as being angry. No one had taught me about the wrath of God, and I hadn't believed or noticed this topic in my time in the Bible. All I could say to her question was, "I don't believe in an angry God."

I wasn't trying to shut down our conversation, but she went quiet on me. We drove in silence to the airport, and when we arrived at the passenger drop-off, she said, "Have a nice life." I had just been excommunicated from *The 700 Club*. Perhaps she sensed that she couldn't get through to me. Maybe she used our time together in silent prayer for my salvation. I do hope to see her again someday and share the good news that Jesus opened my eyes, gave me a new heart, and saved my soul from the wrath of God.

Dr. Todd Miles, who holds a PhD in systematic theology, explained how God's wrath and love are intertwined by pointing to Exodus 34:6–7, when God revealed His glory to Moses. God said, "The LORD, the LORD, a God merciful and gracious, slow to anger, and abounding in steadfast love and faithfulness, keeping steadfast love for thousands, forgiving iniquity and transgression and sin, but who will by no means clear the guilty, visiting the iniquity of the fathers on the children and the children's children, to the third and the fourth generation." Miles said:

> God told Moses that love (*hesed*, a loyal love informed by His particular covenant promises), faithfulness, and mercy character-ize Him. But in the same passage, the Lord explained that He also punishes transgressions and "will by no means clear the guilty."
>
> However the love of God is to be understood, His holiness and commitment to punish the guilty must be taken into consideration. To focus on any one attribute of God to the exclusion of others not only distorts the character of God, but ironically it does not bring one to proper understanding of the attribute in focus. Universalists who elevate the love of God and redefine holiness and justice as an aspect of His love ultimately distort and misunderstand both the divine attribute of love and God in His complex totality.[9]

Some people argue that only the Old Testament God was wrath-ful, and that God in the New Testament / new covenant is a "God of love" without wrath. Again, such a lovely thought, but one that does not stand up biblically. Remember that God's holiness includes love and justice. The word *wrath* appears in the New Testament forty-six times in the King James Version and thirty-six times in the English Standard Version. In most cases, wrath is spoken of in future tense, as in "wrath to come." For example, Romans 5:9 and 1 Thessalonians 1:9–10 show that Jesus is our deliverer from the coming wrath.

In the New Testament, God's judicial wrath is displayed in the eschatological end times that are coming, as we read throughout the book of Revelation. Believers are corrected (Hebrews 12:5–11), and unbelievers will be judged for their sins. Unbelievers will be like people trying to defend themselves in court without attorneys.

Back then, I was spiritually blind. I didn't have the Holy Spirit indwelling me, because I was unsaved, so I didn't receive any conviction for my heretical teachings. I didn't know the Bible, so I had no basis of comparing my teachings against the Word of God. Christians would post warnings to others on my Facebook page, but those comments were always hidden or deleted and the person blocked from further posting. I honestly didn't understand why Christians would oppose my teachings, because I didn't see anything wrong with them. People told me that I was helping them, and said that thanks to my work, they were now talking to God and the angels. I was helping people, so why were Christians mad at me?

At one workshop in remote White Horse, Canada, Christians picketed my event. About twenty men and women with picket signs walked around the building where I held my angel seminar on a cold evening. I went outside to talk with them, because I was completely clueless as to why they'd picket what I was doing. They were quiet, kind, and gentle, which I appreciated. One of the Christians said to me, "We're praying for you and for everyone at this seminar." I was so happy to hear this, because I supposed that their prayers were like my prayers. I sincerely thanked them for praying for me, and they looked surprised. I was so clueless back then, like a spiritual version of Steve Martin in the movie *The Jerk* who thought that everyone was his friend.

Looking back, I can also see how I was insulated by a cocoon of narcissism. People gave me standing ovations after every workshop, and I daily received thank-you letters. Being onstage is weird and tends to inflate the ego if you're not careful, which I wasn't.

Imagine standing onstage, with hundreds of seated people staring at you. These folks have traveled and bought tickets to hear you speak. And every time you say something, they applaud. They laugh at every joke you tell. They continually compliment you and say that you're a gift from God. And they wait for hours in long lines to get your book signed after the event. All this attention gets in your head after a while. You start to believe you're invincible, and you think critics are ill-informed. Don't they *know* who you are? This is what's inside the head and heart of false prophets who get offended when someone points out the biblical truth that refutes their heretical teachings.

I gradually became accustomed to being the center of attention. I'm sure I was obnoxious and ungracious. The public outpouring of anger against my conversion was humbling, and I saw that popularity is fickle and conditional. I am also humbled by going to seminary classes, where I'm the oldest person in classrooms filled with twenty-five-year-old future pastors. I'm an invisible person in these classes, which has been humbling in a healthy and necessary way.

I now pray daily for God to humble me, which is a frightening but necessary prayer. One of my favorite prayers is Psalm 139:23–24:

> Search me, O God, and know my heart!
> Try me and know my thoughts!
> And see if there be any grievous way in me,
> and lead me in the way everlasting!

Since my conversion, I've heard from dozens of Christians who said they'd prayed for me over the years. This includes my brother, Ken, who escaped the Christian Science deception twenty years before I did. Ken had asked each of his men's Bible study groups to pray for me, which makes me cry tears of gratitude even now thinking about his generosity. May this give you encouragement if you are praying for a deceived loved one: keep praying!

Spiritual blindness is a real and pervasive condition. The Bible says that Satan has blinded the minds of those who don't believe in Jesus, so they're unable to see the glorious light of the gospel. The devil puts a veil up so that the gospel is hidden and the Bible isn't understandable to unbelievers (2 Corinthians 4:3–4). The Bible sounds foolish to those who are spiritually blind (1 Corinthians 2:14). The message that Jesus died for our sins on the cross sounds foolish to those who are spiritually blind (1 Corinthians 1:18).

Jesus said:

This is why I speak to them in parables, because seeing they do not see, and hearing they do not hear, nor do they understand. Indeed, in their case the prophecy of Isaiah is fulfilled that says:

You will indeed hear but never understand,
and you will indeed see but never perceive.
For this people's heart has grown dull,
and with their ears they can barely hear,
and their eyes they have closed,
lest they should see with their eyes
and hear with their ears
and understand with their heart
and turn, and I would heal them.

(MATTHEW 13:13–15, REFERENCING ISAIAH 6:9–10)

Part of God's judgment is allowing people to swim in their deception. Just as God further hardened Pharaoh's already hard heart (Exodus 9:12), so, too, does God allow the deceived to remain deceived. As author Justin Peters recently told me, "False teachers are part of God's judgment upon unbelievers."[10] The Bible says that after a while, God allows people to wallow in their sin as part of His judgment (Romans 1:24–32). As difficult as it is to fathom, God used my false teachings in His wrath against me and unbelievers.

As much as I wish I could have been born and raised in a solid Christian upbringing, I can also see God's genius in opening my eyes and pulling me out of the New Age at the peak of my career. At the time of my salvation, my weekly videos were getting 180,000 views each. A lot of people saw my Christian testimony videos, and from the letters I receive, my videos are planting seeds for God's kingdom. God is using my past for His glory!

I was known as "the angel lady" for more than two decades. People in the media and event producers would often introduce me as one of the world's leading experts on angels. I'm only saying this to warn you not to automatically think someone's an expert, even if the media says she is. Be sure to test everything that everyone says against Scripture, to make sure that he or she is speaking God's truth. I didn't know the Bible at that time, so I blame a lot of my heresy on biblical ignorance. After I read the Bible the first time, I was shocked to find that there was no one in the Bible who actually called on an angel, as I'd been teaching. God was the one who sent angels to people, and the person was usually terrified when he or she saw an angel.

My experiences with what I believed were angels, were real experiences. I really saw visions that looked like angels, complete with wings and long gowns. I gave people accurate messages that I'd receive as thoughts, visions, and voices. I did these demonstrations to prove that angels are real. Now I know that we can't trust our experiences as a foundation for our beliefs. We must trust the wisdom that we gain from studying God's Word.

As I mentioned earlier, when I'd give these "angel readings" at my workshops, I'd always notice conservatively dressed people storming out of the building. They were likely Christians who were offended by my heretical statements and actions. I sure wish they would've stayed around and talked with me after the workshop to share the gospel with me. But they never did. My only interactions with Christians were on social media, where they'd post Scripture in the comments below my social media posts. Out of context, though, I didn't understand what the Bible verses they posted were trying to convey. I just thought the Christians were angry with me, so I avoided them out of my fears of conflict. If I could turn back time, I would've asked them to teach me the meaning of those Bible verses.

After all those high-rolling travels, Michael and I would return to our home in Hawaii. We sure seemed to be living the dream! I didn't realize at the time that I was spending money as fast as it came in. That's how the enemy works. He seems to give you your wishes, but then he will make you dependent on him. I didn't realize that at the time, and most people don't. Think about how many rock stars live their lives. They start off as insecure teenagers wanting attention from girls. They practice their music, and some of them seem to be overnight successes. Suddenly there are more girls and more money than they can deal with. They buy big mansions with swimming pools, go on continuous music tours, and live the high life. Often their stories end with them living in squalor as broke, recovering drug addicts.

The enemy is a sugar daddy who'll give you the high life, but you will always feel hungry and want more. That's one of the key characteristics of those who are following the enemy. They are never satisfied. I wasn't. I wanted more followers on Facebook, more book sales, and more beautiful gowns to wear at my events. I was obsessed with material things, and I was also prideful, and I didn't even realize it.

I was also headed straight to hell! And I didn't even believe in hell back then. One of the biggest lies the devil tells us is that he doesn't exist. In the New Age, the belief is there is no evil, no sin, no devil, and no hell. The only thing bad is being negative or unkind. In the New Age, the belief is that if you are a "good person," you will automatically go to heaven.

It's interesting that most New Agers don't believe in hell, but they believe in heaven. That's probably because New Agers don't want to acknowledge anything that they perceive as being harsh or negative. I know, because that's how I was. I couldn't handle any conflict or bad news. I kept my head in the sand like an ostrich. The devil can work under cover in the New Age, because no one is looking for him. New Agers blame politicians and conservatives for the problems in the world, instead of blaming Satan.

SEVEN

Worshiping the Creation
Instead of the Creator

In 2012, Michael and I moved to a home on a hill above Lahaina, on the island of Maui, Hawaii. We had a big ocean view and could see humpback whales spouting from our backyard. The temperature was 82 degrees Fahrenheit daily and would dip to 75 degrees at night. As someone who frequently feels cold, I loved the warmth. At night we'd sit outside, looking at the stars. For some reason, I got it into my head to talk to the stars. I asked the stars to please help our planet stay safe and protected. Talk about misguided prayers! I was talking to the *creation* instead of the *Creator*!

The apostle Paul described God's wrath coming upon someone who did what I did: "because they exchanged the truth about God for a lie and worshiped and served the creature rather than the Creator" (Romans 1:25). It's only by God's mercy and grace that He saved me instead of punishing me, as I deserved.

Living in Hawaii is not as fun or glamorous as staying in a Hawaiian hotel on vacation. The tropics can be challenging for full-time residents.

Yes, the sunsets are gorgeous, the plumeria flowers perfume the warm breezes, and the ocean is warm. Please understand that I'm not putting Hawaii down. I *loved* living there and had planned on living in Hawaii for the rest of my life. I'm just explaining what it's really like to live there, which I did for eleven years on the Big Island and Maui, because it's different from a tropical vacation. When you visit Hawaii as a tourist, you usually stay in a hotel that uses lots of pesticides, so insects and geckos aren't the nuisance that they are for full-time residents.

Before moving to Hawaii, I'd spent a lot of time visiting my friends Angie and Duke at their home in Kona. So I was familiar with the insects of Hawaii before I moved to the islands full-time. First, the Hawaiian cockroaches are big and they have wings and are attracted to light. When you open your door or window at night, the cockroaches fly right in and sometimes hit your head with their armored bodies as they fly around your home in search of food.

Large centipedes that look like creatures from horror monster movies also intrude Hawaiian homes. One time I was sitting in my home office, wearing sandals, and a centipede slithered across the bare top of my foot as I watched in terror. You can't have bed skirts or allow your bedsheets or blankets to drag on the floor, because centipedes will crawl into your bed. That happened to me once in the middle of the night, and the centipede stung my leg with a pain that must've equaled being branded with a scalding iron. *Ouch!*

The other "residents" of Hawaii are the geckos, which look cute and are appreciated for their appetite for gnats and mosquitos. But they leave trails of excrement wherever they go. And of course, the islands, like all tropical locations, are loaded with teeny-tiny flies referred to as "no-see-ums" as well as teeny mosquitoes because they sneakily bite your arms, legs, and face. Even though they're tiny, these flies have the typical, unmistakable, high-pitched sound you can hear as you're falling asleep. Michael and I had a mosquito net around our bed, and we still got bit.

Hurricanes are another challenge in the islands. Sitting out in the remotest area in the world, farther away from any other land mass, Hawaii is vulnerable to hurricanes once or twice a year. Every year there'd be one or more hurricanes poised to slam into the islands. After Hurricane Iniki devastated the Hawaiian island of Kauai in 1992, residents take hurricane threats seriously. Schools shut down, shelters are opened, and grocery store shelves are emptied. It was such a vulnerable feeling enduring the hurricane that passed near Maui in 2015, which sounded and felt like a freight train going through our home.

I'd pray for the hurricanes to miss our islands and for everyone's safety. I'd also pray when hurricanes threatened other areas of the world. My prayers were quite different before I was saved by Jesus, though: I'd visualize a wall of white light surrounding Hawaii, and ask the angels to push away the storm. Whenever the hurricanes missed Hawaii, I'd quietly congratulate myself for my prayers working. This is another clear sign of false prophets: they take credit for God's work. Although I wasn't publicly boasting about my prayers saving the day, as some false prophets do, I was inwardly gloating. It was all glory to Doreen, instead of to God, who rightfully deserves all the glory and praise.

Despite the bugs and hurricanes, living in Hawaii was a wonderful experience. The dazzling sunsets, beautiful birds, fragrant flowers, delicious tropical fruit, and beautiful coral reefs are a testimony to God's creation. Today, such natural beauty reminds me of the psalmist's praises:

> In his hand are the depths of the earth;
> the heights of the mountains are his also.
> The sea is his, for he made it,
> and his hands formed the dry land.
> Oh come, let us worship and bow down;
> let us kneel before the LORD, our Maker!
>
> (PSALM 95:4–6)

You'd think that someone would be happy to be living in Maui with a wonderful husband and family, plenty of friends, a nice ocean-view home, enjoying good health and a successful career. However, without Jesus true joy and peace is impossible. We have a broken relationship with God unless Jesus is our mediator. So I wasn't happy during those years.

I actually got sucked into the world of conspiracy theories while living in Maui. I became obsessed about "the new world order," "chemtrails," and the Illuminati. I was constantly upset about genetically modified foods and politicians who didn't vote as I thought they should.

Now, some of these issues might be legitimate, and I'm not implying that Christians should be passive about world events. However, looking back, I find it ironic that my New Age beliefs were all about seeking peace, and yet I was anything but peaceful. I convinced Michael to spend our money on survival supplies, including two huge and expensive water tanks in our backyard. I was fearfully convinced that some government was going to take over the world, and we'd need to rely on our own supplies to survive. Maybe that's true, and perhaps it's a good idea to prepare, but my point is that I was fearful and angry most days because of my view of the world and its future. As the prophet Isaiah said, "Do not call conspiracy all that this people calls conspiracy, and do not fear what they fear, nor be in dread" (Isaiah 8:12).

When we focus on the world, we'll always be accosted by the worldly situations that are born of sin. Only by keeping our focus on the true King, Jesus, can we find any joy in this world. Welsh Protestant minister and medical doctor David Martyn Lloyd-Jones wrote that Christians who know their Bible should not be surprised at the state of the world as it is.[1] In the New Age, we were obsessed with changing and "saving" the world in a material sense. Yet, only Jesus can save in the spiritual sense of eternal salvation. The Bible tells us that before

Jesus' return the world will worsen, with increased wars and lawlessness (Matthew 24:6–7, 12); drought and famine (Matthew 24:7); earthquakes and other natural disasters (Zechariah 14:4–5; Matthew 24:7; Mark 13:8); plagues and epidemics (Revelation 6:7–8); and a powerful false prophet who practices signs and wonders (2 Thessalonians 2:1–4; 2 Timothy 3:13; Revelation 13:13–14; 19:19–21).

My friend Warren Smith is the author of *False Christ Coming*. Smith's research and writings trace how the prophesied Antichrist is the deceptive behind-the-scenes figure who is orchestrating the whole New Age movement. Smith wrote:

> And his [the Antichrist's] New Age/New Gospel/New Spirituality is now accepted by millions of well-intentioned people around the world. Through his extraordinary use of the mass media, this "Christ" has presented his New Spirituality through a small but powerful network of key people who enthusiastically proclaim his teachings. Convinced their "Christ" is the true Christ, most of those in the network seem to be unaware of his *real* identity. While the network front line is eagerly mainstreaming the New Age Gospel, this "Christ" has been able to remain in the background, overseeing his Peace Plan to birth a new humanity—a new humanity that will be empowered by his spirit, committed to his teachings, and from which he will one day *emerge*.[2]

It's grievous to believe now that I was once one of those in that "select network" that Smith wrote about, enthusiastically proclaiming and mainstreaming the false New Age teachings of this Antichrist figure. During my extended time of involvement, I really believed the "Christ" I was following was the true Christ, not the false Christ (Antichrist) figure warned about in the Bible.

What awful irony! I'd been an integral part of the spiritual deception that the true Christ warned would come in His name! And I had been one of the Bible's warned-about false teachers as I brought this false gospel to anyone who'd listen. I was very sincere, but I was sincerely deceived. But now, with the Bible in hand and the true Christ in my heart, I plan on being deceived no more.

Martyn Lloyd-Jones also captured the reason for my unhappiness before salvation: "Whenever you put happiness before righteousness, you will be doomed to misery. That is the great message of the Bible from beginning to end. They alone are truly happy who are seeking to be righteous."[3] Righteousness means having a right relationship with God and other people. We can't attain righteousness by ourselves, but only through Jesus' crucifixion and our faith in Him (2 Corinthians 5:21). On the cross, Jesus took the punishment we deserved, and He imputed His righteousness to us. The happiness I sought could only come through having a restored relationship with God, through the sacrifice that Jesus made on our behalf.

Little did I realize at the time that Jesus was pursuing me out of the New Age. While driving around Maui, I'd listen to the Christian Satellite Network (CSN), which had a clear radio signal and interesting sermons. I still identified as a Christian, and I was very interested in anything related to Jesus. I just didn't have discernment filters on, so I'd listen to a sermon from a solid Bible teacher equally as I would from a New Age teacher claiming to channel some spirit. I still couldn't distinguish true from false teachings.

A big part of my salvation happened while driving and listening to a radio sermon by Alistair Begg on January 14, 2015, called "Itching Ears" from his Guard the Truth series. With his melodic Scottish accent, Pastor Begg discussed "itching ears," a topic with which I was unfamiliar. He quoted 2 Timothy 4:3–4: "For the time is coming when people will not endure sound teaching, but having itching ears they will accumulate for themselves teachers to suit their own passions, and will turn away from listening to the truth and wander off into myths."

Pastor Begg began the program with this prayer:

Father, we pray that as we turn to the Bible, that you will open our eyes and grant to us understanding in our minds, and faith and trust. Accomplish your purpose as we pray, for Jesus' sake, amen.[4]

Well, the prayer worked, because the program pierced through the darkness of my deception. Pastor Begg explained that in the end times, people wouldn't want sound doctrine but would instead want their ears tickled with feel-good and me-centered messages. They wouldn't want to hear the gospel. When Pastor Begg said that, I turned up the radio volume. I didn't quite comprehend his message then compared to when I relisten to the broadcast now. All his talk about sin went straight over my head, because I was raised to believe there's no such thing as sin "in spiritual truth" and that I was perfect, whole, and complete no matter what because I was made in God's image and likeness. So, I couldn't be saved until I recognized my sinful nature, which wouldn't occur for another two years.

However, that January day in 2015, when Pastor Begg explained the importance of not giving people messages of false hope, my wall of deception began to crack. His warning against "false hope" got through to me! As I drove along, I realized that I'd been offering false-hope messages to people through my books and cards about angels. I'd even had a woman on Facebook chide me about a post where I'd written, "Don't worry about going through dark times, as there's always light at the end of the tunnel." She'd commented, "Really? Are you sure about this, Doreen?" Her simple remark peeled something away within me, and when I heard the sermon about false hope, *I really heard the message.* I hope to thank Pastor Begg someday for his "Itching Ears" sermon, and also express gratitude for his other sermons and books that continue to edify me to this day.

I hadn't been trying to pacify people with false-hope messages. It was my belief that if you had hope and positive thoughts, something good would happen. Yet in that sermon, I learned that God doesn't always will happy endings as we define them. We see this principle in the story of the blind man healed by Jesus. When Jesus first met the blind man, the disciples asked who had sinned—the man or his parents—to cause the man to be born blind. Jesus replied that the man's condition was not a result of sin, but so that "the works of God might be displayed in him" (John 9:1–3). Like the blind man whom Jesus healed, sometimes we suffer expressly to bring glory to God. Other times, our suffering is to motivate us to get on our knees, repent, and return to God.

Yet, I admit that I was also a "people pleaser" who wanted my audience members to feel happy and hopeful. So, I would sugarcoat my messages until Pastor Begg's sermon confronted me. In fact, Pastor Paul Washer wrote, "One of the greatest distinguishing marks of a false prophet is that he will always tell you what you want to hear."[5]

As I listened to Pastor Begg's sermon, I made a conscious decision to stop giving hope unless I was 100 percent certain. I later learned that the false prophets in biblical times also gave messages of false hope. The prophet Jeremiah had to deal with these false prophets on a few occasions. Jeremiah was chosen to be God's prophet before he was born (Jeremiah 1:5), and because he was so filled with sorrow at the messages God delivered through him, Jeremiah was known as "the weeping prophet."

Like the other true prophets', Jeremiah's main job was to tell the Israelites to repent from their sins and to become obedient to God. Jeremiah had to warn the Israelites that if they didn't repent, they'd be cast into Babylonian exile for seventy years and Jerusalem would be ruined by invaders. As with most of the true prophets, no one listened to him, and all Jeremiah's prophecies of Jerusalem's ruin and Israel's exile into Babylon came true (Jeremiah 52:12–13).

I used to think that a prophet was the same as a psychic, who would tell you about your soul mate, life purpose, and other personal details. But a biblical true prophet was "God's prosecuting attorney," because he had the unsavory task of telling the Israelites that they'd violated their covenant agreement with the Lord. Biblical true prophets didn't give people "personal readings"; they warned people of God's coming wrath if they didn't obey (Jeremiah 29:10–11).

While Jeremiah was delivering these warnings, false prophets were simultaneously telling people what they wanted to hear. The false prophets were saying that the Israelites had nothing to worry about, because God would never allow anything bad to happen to Jerusalem, where the temple was. The false prophets also accepted money in exchange for these "itching ear" false hope reports, where they'd tell the Israelites that if there was an exile, it would only last two years. Jeremiah accused the false prophets of leading the people of Israel astray, because they were prophesying from Baal (the pagan deity to whom they'd sacrifice infants; Jeremiah 23:13).[6] So the false prophets were getting their messages from the devil, not from God.

God said that He'd never spoken to these false prophets: "I did not send the prophets, yet they ran; I did not speak to them, yet they prophesied" (Jeremiah 23:21). That means the false prophets were getting their messages from their imaginations or from the devil.

God also warned the Israelites not to listen to the false hope messages of these false prophets: "Do not listen to the words of the prophets who prophesy to you, filling you with vain hopes. They speak visions of their own minds, not from the mouth of the LORD. They say continually to those who despise the word of the LORD, 'It shall be well with you'; and to everyone who stubbornly follows his own heart, they say, 'No disaster shall come upon you'" (Jeremiah 23:16–17). Although the false prophets were telling the Israelites they had nothing to worry about, disaster was about to strike. If people had listened to Jeremiah—a *true* prophet of the Lord—they might've repented or at least been prepared for the Babylonian sieges and exile.

I was starting to realize that I was a false prophet when I heard that Alistair Begg radio sermon. Still, I wasn't reading my Bible and I continued to teach New Age heresy. Oh, I was a tough nut to crack: a completely spiritually blind false prophet who believed she was a Christian helping God save the world.

EIGHT

The False Christ
of the New Age

One way to know if we're on the path of deception is by monitoring our spiritual and emotional hunger levels. If there's a gnawing emptiness that we're desperate to fill, that's a sign we're dining on spiritual junk food instead of on the main course of daily Bible reading and prayer. The hollow promises of deception guarantee that we'll stay on the hamster wheel of seeking and never finding.

Deception is like a progressive disease: We may start out innocently enough with consulting an iffy, Christian-like "spiritual healer" because we're desperate for health. Or perhaps we're single and want reassurance that we will meet our spouse, so we consult "angel cards" that seem to be safe because, after all, the Bible has angels. Or we may peek at our horoscope to see what kind of a day is ahead, instead of praying for God to guide our day.

Once we take the bait of these entry points, our appetite for more excitement, experience, and enlightenment takes over. It's like having one potato chip or chocolate candy: you want more. Though you don't realize it, the devil slowly puts blinders over your heart and eyes, and all your prayers shift to you saying, "Give me more, Lord," instead of "Your will, not mine."

There's a saying among alcoholics that's applicable to the dark road of spiritual deception too: "One is too many, and a thousand not enough." This refers to alcoholics needing to completely abstain from drinking. If they have even one sip of alcohol, they may relapse into drinking binges. One drink is too many, because it may trigger relapses that not even one thousand drinks can satiate.

Only Jesus can satiate what we hunger for! Jesus said, "I am the bread of life; whoever comes to me shall not hunger, and whoever believes in me shall never thirst" (John 6:35). If you feel lonely, empty, unloved, or unlovable, please go get on your knees right now and pray for Jesus to lift you up and fill you up.

I learned this the hard way. Right before my salvation, I was at the pinnacle of my New Age career. I enjoyed everything that this world can offer, yet I was still searching and seeking.

Have you ever felt this way? Do you believe that being famous will make you happy? I was the top-selling New Age author and I still wasn't happy. I'd receive standing ovations at my workshops and had millions of social media followers, yet I was still seeking the key to happiness.

Do you believe a relationship will make you happy? I was still searching for happiness, despite having a wonderful relationship with Michael (it's much better now with Jesus at the center and foundation of our marriage).

I had a fifty-acre ranch in Hawaii, a steady income, friends, family, good health—you name it. What I didn't have back then was the real Jesus, whom we meet in the Bible. I had the false Jesus, whom you meet in a New Age meditation or energy healing session.

Only our relationship with our triune God gives us meaning and purpose. Only through Jesus is our hunger satisfied and our thirst quenched. This knowledge gives us true and lasting joy and peace (John 4:14; 6:35; 14:27; 15:11).

Tragically, though, I believed I *did* have a relationship with Jesus back then! Being raised in a false, Christian-like religion gave me the impression that I was a Christian. We used Christian terminology, celebrated the Christian holidays, had a Bible, and up until early adulthood I went to church every Sunday and Wednesday night for church testimonial meetings.

I loved Jesus! The trouble was that I was unknowingly following a *false* Jesus. Christ Himself warned us this would happen in the end times when He said, "For false christs and false prophets will arise and perform great signs and wonders, so as to lead astray, if possible, even the elect" (Matthew 24:24; Mark 13:22).

The false Jesus says that you can do whatever you want as long as you stay happy and positive. He never discusses sin, hell, or repentance. In fact, the false Jesus contradicts what the true Jesus Christ said in the Bible. This false Jesus applauds your every move and says that you can do no wrong because he loves you. You can have as much alcohol, drugs, food, and as many relationships as you'd like. You can try every New Age and occultic practice, worship deity statues, and believe any religion that you want. *Just stay positive*, is his only condition. He also counsels you, "Oh, and stay away from those 'negative people' who are trying to convince you to read your Bible or go to church."

If that sounds like the Jesus you're following—especially if you "met" him in a New Age meditation or energy healing session—please get on your knees and pray for God's help in following the true Jesus. Then start studying the Gospels in the Bible, especially the red letters of Jesus' words.

Because I'd only read small sections of the Bible and was heavily influenced by the false teachings of Christian Science and the New Age (particularly the book called *A Course in Miracles*, which I studied for about twenty years), I held a false view of Jesus. In my mind, Jesus was all-accepting of everyone and everything. He was like a cuddly teddy bear, always approving of whatever we do, as long as we're happy and positive (I equated positivity with having faith back then).

That's why I couldn't understand why Christians seemed so judgmental. I thought, *Well, Jesus never judged anyone, so why were His followers judging people?* I twisted the meaning of "Judge not, that you be not judged" (Matthew 7:1), mistakenly believing this meant to never judge anyone or anything. Many New Age books and teachers teach "relativism," that there is no absolute good or evil. Everything is relative, and nothing is either good or bad unless you think it is, according to the New Age.

I hadn't read the other passages in which Jesus taught about judgment, such as John 7:24: "Do not judge by appearances, but judge with right judgment." That means to judge when something is a sin against God, as Jesus did when He cleared the temple. We are to judge false teachings, as Jesus did when He confronted the Pharisees.

In the New Age, I viewed Jesus as being like Mister Rogers, who told everyone, "I love you just the way you are!" Well, Jesus certainly didn't accept everyone's sinful behavior.

It's true that Jesus spent time with tax collectors, prostitutes, and other sinners, but He didn't say their actions were acceptable. When asked why He was dining with sinners, Jesus replied that healthy people didn't need physicians; only sick people do. He meant that sinners needed Him more than repentant believers did. So He spent time with sinners to help them turn away from sin, repent, and be saved (Matthew 9:12; Mark 2:17; Luke 5:31).

Jesus also told the woman caught in adultery, "Go and sin no more" (John 8:11 NKJV). Jesus confronted sin and false teachings in ways that could be considered harsh today, because Jesus was incapable of lying.

I understand people who fantasize that Jesus was all-accepting of everything and everyone, because that was my definition of love back then too. All it takes is reading the book of Matthew in the Bible to learn that this fantasy is not based in biblical reality.

I also had this disconnect of believing that I was a Christian, but not like *those* Christians. I referred to myself as "an open-minded Christian." I thought that "true Christians" were always peaceful, gentle, and accepting. If someone spoke up about a false teaching, I judged that person as not being a "true Christian."

It's so ironic that before I was saved, I used to judge Christians as being judgmental. The irony was lost on me until the first time I was called a judgmental Christian when I was only trying to help someone.

For example, I was convinced that Jann, my Christian sister-in-law, was judging me. For years I avoided her. The first time I was with Jann after Jesus saved me, I started to cry because I realized that my sister-in-law hadn't been judging me all those years. She had simply tried to help me, but I was blind and deaf to her help. Now she and I are sisters in Christ.

All those wasted years, though! It makes me weep to recall how spiritually blind and deceived I was before Jesus opened my eyes. I pray that reading my story may inspire someone to study the Bible.

A lot of New Age practices are borrowed from other cultures, like a spiritual buffet of trying a bit of this and that. During my time in the New Age, I engaged in spiritual ceremonies, practices, and workshops related to the following cultures:

- **Native American shamanism**, such as "sweat lodges," where you sit with other people in a closed tent with hot steaming coals inside, until you hallucinate from lack of oxygen. This is called "a vision quest" or "journeying," and it often involves taking psychedelic plants to induce visions that supposedly answer your quest for guidance. Other practices included "drumming circles," with people standing or dancing next to each other in a big circle while banging on handheld drums and chanting. These drumming circles were viewed as therapeutic, cathartic, and ways to worship the full moon, manifest your desires, or conjure rain. In addition, we used dried sagebrush to "smudge" away "lower energy" (the New Age term for negativity or evil spirits).

- **Hinduism** and **Buddhism**, including yoga, which teaches poses that were originally designed to bow down and worship deities. During yoga sessions, you'll hear people use words in the ancient Eastern language called Sanskrit, especially the heretical pantheistic term *namaste*, which means, "The god in me recognizes and honors the god within you." In the New Age, it's also common to have Buddha and Hindu deity statues and symbols in your home, and to wear these images on your clothing and jewelry. In addition, New Agers often wear clothing related to other cultures, especially Bohemian looks with block prints and mirrored fabric from India as a throwback to the 1970s fashions popularized when the Beatles took meditation classes in India. New Age also involves Eastern forms of meditation, such as chanting mantras, meditating on the Buddha, emptying your mind, and meditative walking. In addition, New Agers study and practice Eastern "energy healing" techniques, such as qigong, which involves imagining energy balls in your hands that you send to others. Christian meditation is quite different, as it involves Bible reading and prayer.

- **Celtic, Gaelic, and Druid** practices, including worshiping Celtic goddesses and celebrating ancient Celtic holy days, such as Beltane (a fertility May Day springtime ritual), Ostara (also a fertility springtime festival, associated with eggs and rabbits), Samhain (pronounced Sau-ehn, it's the occultic precursor to modern Halloween celebrations), and Yule (a winter nature festival that many New Agers practice as a rejection of Christian Christmas).

These cultures are viewed as being cooler and deeper in meaning compared to traditional Christian values. People who practice these New Age methods are seen as knowledgeable, awake, and aware, whereas traditional Christian celebrations are seen as dry, boring, and unaware by most New Agers. I was amazed after being saved to discover how rich, deep, and exciting traditional Christian ceremonies can be. I now *love* going to our Baptist church!

The Gospels

That dream with Grandma Pearl about Pythagoras (chapter 2) had led me to study Egyptian spirituality, including tarot cards. That resulted in my creating several decks of "angel cards." I wanted to make cards that were similar to tarot but without the symbols and words that had frightened me.

I'd made angel cards with beautiful images licensed from artists and with positive words on each card since New Age spirituality is all about positivity. The words on each card may have been positive and encouraging, but they were also unbiblical. They gave false hope (for example, "The worst is now behind you," "Everything will be better soon") and encouraged self-glory instead of God-glory (such as "Believe in yourself," "You deserve the best," etc.).

The booklets accompanying each card deck also contained heretical teachings based on New Age deception about Jesus as "an ascended master," encouragement to pray to angels, and false assurances that the cards were spiritually safe. I sincerely apologize to anyone who was misled by these cards, as that was never my intention. Before Jesus opened my eyes and I began studying the Bible, I believed in those cards and used them myself.

The decks consisted of forty-four cards because I was fascinated by Pythagorean numerology and was convinced that fours signified the Holy Trinity (three) plus one for the angels. I know, I know: it's beyond blasphemy. But that's how deceived I was back then.

Lots of people said they were attracted to my books and cards because I used Christian terminology. My previous work is a prime example of why we can't trust someone just because she says she's a Christian, uses Christian terms, or quotes the Bible. I thought I was trustworthy back then, but now I see that I was a wretched false prophet. Such a sinner! God is filled with mercy and grace to save me, considering how much heresy I spread worldwide. Well, I deeply pray that this book can help clean up some of the mess I created.

The cards sold very well from the beginning. Major department stores sold them, and celebrities used them in their television shows and posted them on social media. Because of the popularity of my angel cards, and because I spoke about Jesus in my teachings (the false Jesus, but no one knew that unless he or she had studied Scripture), people asked me to create a deck of cards with Jesus images. Even at the height of my deception, I cringed at this request. I had enough respect for Jesus to know I couldn't make a deck of cards with His image.

That all changed when I came across the paintings of a Mormon artist who portrayed Jesus as I imagined Jesus to appear: with a warm smile and twinkling eyes. The artist and I decided to collaborate on these cards. Although I was an outrageous heretic, I still had some limits. So, instead of channeling Jesus messages for the cards, as I normally did with angel messages for the angel cards, I felt strongly that I should extract Jesus' words from the Gospels in the Bible. That was one of the best decisions I could have made—or that God steered me to make!

I opened my red-letter New King James Bible and began searching for Jesus' words to match each of the card illustrations. For example, I paired "Knock, and it will be opened to you" (Matthew 7:7 NKJV) with a painting of Jesus knocking on a door.

Although I'd previously *listened* to audios of the Gospels, this was my first time *reading* the entire Gospels of Matthew, Mark, Luke, and John. Some of my Christian friends wonder how I could've listened to Christian broadcasts all those years and still remained unsaved. The reason was that I never identified as a sinner who needed saving. I was so insulated by Christian Science and New Age doctrine, which denied human depravity, that the words "Jesus died for our sins" went over my head. I was certain I wasn't a sinner. I was a "good person."

That's why it's important to avoid false prophets who claim to be sinless or who teach "sinless perfection" doctrine. I used to be personally insulted when someone called me a sinner. Now I realize that we're all sinners, as Paul explained in Romans 3:23: "All have sinned and fall short of the glory of God." The apostle John, one of the closest companions to Jesus during His earthly ministry, said that we are liars if we claim we have no sin: "If we say we have no sin, we deceive ourselves, and the truth is not in us. If we confess our sins, he is faithful and just to forgive us our sins and to cleanse us from all unrighteousness. If we say we have not sinned, we make him a liar, and his word is not in us" (1 John 1:8–10). When God saves us, we still spontaneously have sinful thoughts (such as anger, envy, lust, lack of loving God), and we may even engage in sinful actions. The big difference is that *we don't want to sin* when we're saved, whereas before salvation we didn't care much about God's opinion. After salvation, we hopefully repent and stop sinful actions, such as adultery, lying, and stealing. It's not realistic, however, to believe that we'll be completely sin-free this side of heaven. It's also dishonest for a teacher to claim to have no sinful thoughts. Does that person *really* love God and everyone wholeheartedly at every moment of every day? If not, then he or she has sinned by breaking the commandments that Jesus said were the greatest (Matthew 22:36–39). Upon these two commandments, all the Law and the Prophets hang (Matthew 22:40).

As I read the Gospels while looking for verses for my Jesus cards, my eyes were being opened to the truth. My old worldviews of Jesus being an all-inclusive, anything-goes buddy were shattering. Then when I read Mark 8:31, my beliefs about Jesus were turned upside down. In this passage, Jesus plainly foretold His death and resurrection. Peter's eyes were opened to Jesus' true identity as the prophesied Messiah, but he tried to rebuke Jesus to turn away from the cross. Jesus in turn rebuked Peter and explained to His disciples the high cost of following Him, saying that whoever wanted to follow Him needed to take up their cross and deny themselves (Mark 8:27–37).[1] Next came verse 38, which helped to open my own eyes to Jesus:

> "For whoever is ashamed of me and of my words in this adulterous and sinful generation, of him will the Son of Man also be ashamed when he comes in the glory of his Father with the holy angels."

I set the Bible aside, closed my eyes, and tried to grasp what I'd just read. Did Jesus—whom I'd always seen as accepting of everyone and everything—say that He'd be ashamed of me if I was too ashamed to talk about Him to my audiences, readers, friends, and family?

I recalled the times when audiences pushed back as I'd mention Jesus. I'd hear a collective inhale from audience members, and some would even storm out. Others would crisply correct me: "His name's not Jesus; it's Yeshua!" or "Don't call him Jesus; he's Sananda!" (Sananda is the New Age term for Jesus.) The point is that the name of Jesus triggered them. I also believe the name triggers the demons who are oppressing New Agers. After all, we read in Matthew 8:29 and Luke 4:41 about demons shouting when they saw Jesus.

Many people enter the New Age because something upset them with church or Christianity. Perhaps they felt judged or met a hypocritical church member. Or they understandably recoiled at hearing about a pastor having an affair or a priest abusing a child. Some people turn to the New Age because they don't like rules, which they call "dogma," and they want to engage in sinful activities without feeling judged. The New Age falsely teaches that people can do whatever they want with whomever they want. In the New Age, this is called freedom, but New Agers don't realize it's actually slavery to sinful addictions.

Some enter the New Age because they're bored with Christianity. Perhaps they grew up in the church and are tired of hearing the same Bible stories repeated. Their youth groups may have offered superficial entertainment instead of answering their questions about life. There's also a psychological process called "habituation," which happens when you stop noticing a familiar environment. For example, do you notice your sofa when you walk into your living room? The phenomenon of habituation also occurs when people work in a bakery and no longer notice the aroma of freshly baked cookies. Our brain is wired to notice what is novel and unusual and to tune out what is familiar and ordinary.

Sadly, some people habituate to their church environment. They no longer feel passion when singing hymns, and they forget to feel grateful for what Jesus did on the cross. The New Age, in contrast, seems to offer novelty, mystical experiences, and adrenaline rushes with its drumming circles, yoga classes, and freedom of expression. There are very few rules in the New Age (except for staying positive), which feels refreshing to those leaving fundamentalist churches. Temptations abound to enter the New Age, but it's like a mouse trap that's hard to leave after you fall for its bait.

Because of audience pushback, I'd reduced the times when I discussed Jesus at workshops or in videos or books. Reading that Jesus would be ashamed of me in Mark 8:38 (and repeated in Luke 9:26) brought up fear about my eternity, which I'd never before doubted. In the New Age, you only pay attention to near-death experience (NDE) testimonies that say everyone's invited to heaven. I'm convinced the devil orchestrates some of these NDEs to con people into believing in universalism and pluralism.

After hearing the Alistair Begg radio seminar about false prophets tickling ears with incorrect teachings, and reading Mark 8:38 about Jesus being ashamed of me, I became aware of the Holy Spirit's convictions. I began mentioning Jesus more often, although I still didn't understand the gospel or Jesus' true identity. I started emphasizing that we don't worship or pray to angels but only give glory to God. As I said, I wasn't a rebellious Christian; I was just ignorant of true theology. I did my best to teach from my evolving worldview. In retrospect, I should've stopped teaching and studied the Bible for a few years. But I had a full workshop schedule and the narcissistic belief that I had to keep going.

NINE

Church Shopping

"I want to go to church," I said to my husband. "A regular Christian church, not a New Age church." I was hungry to learn more about Jesus and the Bible.

Over the years, I'd tried to blend New Age beliefs with Christianity. I'd attended various religious services and ceremonies over the years, celebrating them all because of the New Age belief of coexistence. You've probably seen the bumper sticker of the various religious symbols side by side with the message that "we're all worshiping the same God." This goes along with a similar New Age belief that "all paths lead to heaven," and my favorite tagline was "The more friends you have in heaven, the better," which meant that I prayed to Jesus along with deities of other religions. Exclusivity just didn't fit with my worldview that God and Jesus accept everyone equally. I had a lot to learn about God's love and holiness.

My husband was raised in the Methodist Church and had been baptized at age twelve. However, he and his family had fallen away from church attendance, and Michael had developed his own theology. He loved Jesus and was more familiar with the Bible than I was, but he also held decidedly New Age beliefs. He traveled with me to New Age workshops, where he was onstage with me, playing meditative keyboard music. Michael frequently taught New Age doctrine from the stage and gave psychic readings to audience members. At my book signings, people stood in line to ask Michael questions, and he'd happily counsel them from a New Age–Christian blended worldview.

Like me, Michael tried to mix New Age with Christianity. Yet, like oil and water, Christianity and New Age can never mix. In the appendix of this book, I list the reasons why this is so. The main difference, though, is that the New Age is all about glorifying and empowering yourself, while Christianity is about glorifying God and praising Him for His power.

My point is that Michael and I were *both* involved in the New Age deception. Some people have insinuated that Michael manipulated me into Christianity. These rumors usually originate from people who can't accept or understand my conversion. The truth is that Jesus was pulling both Michael and me out of the New Age simultaneously.

We began shopping for a church to attend. We started at a Pentecostal Foursquare church. We loved the pastor, a warm and loving man named Sione, which in his native Tongan means "God is gracious." Pastor Sione would only preach for ten or fifteen minutes each service because his wife was convinced the congregation didn't want to hear him talk much longer. Michael and I wanted to hear him, though! The rest of the two-hour services were devoted to worship music, prayer requests, and praise reports. Those are all worthy uses of service time, but Michael and I wanted longer sermons.

We tried various churches. In Hawaii, where we lived, choices for everything—schools, restaurants, stores, and churches—are limited because the islands are only so big. So there weren't as many churches from which to choose, compared to a mainland city. Many of the church services were in the native Hawaiian language, which we found beautifully charming. We did our best to understand Hawaiian, but it was challenging to learn theology in a different language.

Finally, we landed at an Episcopal church. My longtime friend Becky, who'd grown up Episcopalian, was certain that I'd like the church. Many people have put me down for attending the Episcopal Church, as it is liberal. Let me just say that the Episcopal Church was a soft landing place for me after coming out of the New Age. I couldn't have handled a conservative church, like the one we now attend, after a lifetime of deception. Pastor Chris Rosebrough said the Episcopal Church was my "halfway house," where I could detox from the New Age.[1]

I'm also grateful for the support that my pastors and the church administrators at the Episcopal church gave me during my time of intense persecution. A New Age woman who was angry about my conversion began frequently calling and writing the church, and the bishop's office, to cuss at them because I was attending their church. They handled this spiritual warfare with grace and concern for my welfare, and I am deeply grateful. Since that time, I've had to be more cautious about publicly saying what church or school I'm attending.

From the beginning of our attendance until the day we moved away, Michael and I were warmly welcomed by the Episcopalians, who have a well-earned reputation for being friendly and hospitable. Within weeks of our first church visit, Michael and I were volunteering on various church committees and making friends.

I attended the women's Bible study monthly meetings, where we studied the women of the Bible. Michael and I also attended a coed Bible study and a few other classes, including catechism to join the church. I was disappointed, though, when I heard our coed Bible teacher say the Bible was errant, and class members expressed disbelief that parts of the Bible were authentic. Fortunately, God had a way to help me trust that His Word is God-breathed (2 Timothy 3:16).

When Jesus Changed My Life

January 7, 2017, I attended an outdoor Saturday afternoon service at our Episcopal church. That day changed my life and eternal destiny forever. It was the beginning of the service, when announcements were read. We hadn't prayed yet, my eyes were open, and I was 100 percent sober, as I had been for more than a decade. My point is that the experience I'm about to describe wasn't influenced by intoxicants.

During the announcements, a church member who was moving out of the area was recognized for her valuable volunteerism while she'd been a congregant. As I watched this woman, I was struck by how pure and natural she seemed. She received appreciation from all of us with what appeared to be genuine humility.

Just then, she—and everything around her—faded from view, and I saw an overwhelmingly bright light! The rays of this light moved outwardly in all directions. The light emanated from the heart of a dark-haired man wearing a white linen-like robe, whom I instantly identified as Jesus. He didn't move or talk, and it wasn't as if He was personally connecting with me alone. I had the sense that Jesus was there for all of us, all of the time.

I believe that I momentarily glimpsed Jesus in heaven that day. I also believe that God is sovereign and so can use any means He chooses to bring about salvation. I'd been having visions since childhood, so it's logical that God used a vision as the means of saving me. After all, a vision of Jesus' light saved and transformed the apostle Paul (Acts 9:3) and Stephen saw God's glory and Jesus before his death (Acts 7:55–56), so my experience didn't contradict Scripture.

Since that day I've only had two other visions, and now I don't have visions at all because I don't need them. I'm also now cautious when people tell me about their visions, because I know the visions I had in the New Age were instigated by demons. These days when I have intuitive feelings, I immediately hand them to God and trust Him to lead me.

People have asked me whether I could've seen a demon masquerading as Jesus that day. Well, it's *possible,* but since the vision led me out of the New Age and into Christianity, that demon should be fired from his job. As Jesus said to the Pharisees when they thought He partnered with Beelzebub (Satan) to cast out demons, "Every kingdom divided against itself is brought to desolation, and every city or house divided against itself will not stand" (Matthew 12:25 NKJV; Luke 11:17). In other words, the devil doesn't work against himself by evangelizing people into Christianity.

My vision also reminds me of the reports from Muslims who have dreams or visions of a "man in a white robe," which leads them to embrace Christianity. Tom Doyle, author of *Dreams and Visions: Is Jesus Awakening the Muslim World?,* found that some Muslims' dreams point them to a specific person. They meet that person soon after having the dream, and that person turns out to be a Christian evangelizer who leads the Muslim to study the Bible and convert to Christianity.

At the end of his book, Doyle assessed whether these dreams and visions are aligned with the conversion vision of the apostle Paul. Doyle interviewed the former Muslims who'd had these dreams and found they could remember concrete details of the vision years later. These dreams and visions didn't result in instant, overnight conversions, but pointed them to Bible study to gain a solid foundation for a true understanding and commitment to Jesus as our Lord and Savior.[2]

Darren Carlson, who holds a PhD from the London School of Theology, has also researched these modern-day visions and dreams that lead to Christian conversions. In an article for the Gospel Coalition, Carlson found a study reported in *Mission Frontiers* that out of 600 Muslim converts, 25 percent experienced a dream that led to their conversion. He also quoted a 2007 study of 750 former Muslims, some of whom converted to Christianity because of a dream they believed to be from God.

While some of my cessationist friends will bristle at this part of the book, having been on the receiving end of a life-changing vision of Jesus that resulted in my conversion, I can say that this is a topic worth investigating. No one wants to be deceived by a demon pretending to be an angel (2 Corinthians 11:14), but we also need to acknowledge that our sovereign God uses *means* to save us.

As Carlson concluded: "Would Satan cast out Satan? Would he give dreams filled with Scripture, pointing to Jesus, that ultimately lead to conversion and purity? I doubt it. . . . Of course Satan tries to attack and muddle what is real, but this should cause us to be discerning, not dismissive."[3]

What stands out about that experience on January 7, 2017, is the light, and also the four realization epiphanies that accompanied the vision. The bright light extended out from the man's heart area. This light seemed to originate from within his chest, shining as moving rays and points of light emanating from the center. The light rays extended to everyone sitting in the congregation, and I was pushed back in my chair by its palpable force. As I mentioned, this didn't seem to be a personal visit from Jesus, but a momentary glimpse into heaven.

The Four Realizations

During that glimpse, though, something extremely important happened in the form of four realizations that occurred, one after another in succession. These were legitimate epiphanies, a term that means insights that help you suddenly realize a deep spiritual truth. It's like a divine download as knowledge appears in your mind. I was, and still remain, completely convinced of the truth of these four realizations:

1. Jesus of the Bible Is Real

My vision was accompanied by a dramatic change in my heart and head toward Jesus. Before that moment, I thought of Him as a mortal man leading us by good example (because my Christian Science upbringing had taught me this), and I had adopted the New Age belief that Jesus was "an ascended master," a term for deities like Buddha and Krishna who were thought to be helping humanity from heaven like a superhero team.

All those misconceptions melted away as I gasped and realized that what I'd read in the Gospels was true: *Jesus really was fully God and fully human during His earthly ministry!* He really is seated at the right hand of our Father in heaven. Jesus performed all those miracles, including walking on water and raising the dead. No one else has been able to do these things except for Jesus. There are no words to adequately explain how this realization blew my mind, except to say that my heretical worldviews of fifty-eight years were instantly replaced with Christian theology.

2. The Bible Is True

In that moment, I knew with absolute certainty—and still do today—that the Bible is inerrant and trustworthy. I was previously swayed by New Age conspiracy theories that claimed the Bible was tampered with by Constantine and the Roman Catholic Church for manipulative, nefarious reasons.

I didn't need to consult with apologists (people who defend the Christian faith and inerrancy of the Bible), as I knew for certain that the Bible is God's Word. Since that time, though, I've read fascinating biblical archaeological work supporting my epiphany. I especially recommend the writings and videos of Daniel B. Wallace, the executive director of the Center for the Study of New Testament Manuscripts.

3. Jesus Really Did Die for Our Sins

This epiphany was another 180-degree turnaround from my previous worldview, which had denied the existence of sin and believed the fall was a myth (from Christian Science and New Age influences).

Before January 7, 2017, I couldn't wrap my mind around the phrase, "Jesus died for your sins." I didn't understand why anyone would have to die, especially Jesus. I also didn't believe that I'd sinned, as my influences of Christian Science, the New Age, and *A Course in Miracles* said that the only sin is negative thinking. I didn't identify as a sinner, because I didn't understand the nature and gravity of sin.

My false beliefs unraveled as I had this epiphany. It was as if I could feel the extreme weight of humanity's sins and God's wrath striking Jesus' crucified body like agonizing arrows. Of course, I felt only a fraction of the weight and the suffering Jesus endured on the cross to save us.

This realization radically transformed my beliefs. You see, New Agers generally hold to a documentary called *Zeitgeist*, which gives unfounded opinions that the crucifixion is a story borrowed from ancient Sumerian and Egyptian mythology. While there's not one shred of evidence to support *Zeitgeist*, the documentary is compelling because of its dramatic music, voice-over, and visual effects. When you're in the New Age, you don't want Christianity to be true because then you'd have to stop committing sinful behaviors.

In addition to the *Zeitgeist* documentary, the book *A Course in Miracles*, which claims to be channeled from Jesus, also denies the crucifixion. This book is often referred to as "the New Age bible" because so many New Agers read it religiously, as I did for twenty years.

The realization that Jesus died for our sins led me to repentance and salvation when I finally understood my sinful nature after reading Deuteronomy 18:10–12, which lists sins I'd been committing, such as fortune-telling, divination, mediumship, and interpreting omens. When I read that God finds people who practice these methods "detestable" and "an abomination," I fell to my knees crying. Before that moment, I thought my New Age work was helping God save the world. Reading the Bible told me that Jesus is our Savior, not me. God didn't need me; I needed God.

4. I Needed to Leave the New Age

The fourth and final realization was a directive, like a loving but firm command: "You need to leave the New Age." It was time. There wasn't an option to agree or disagree with this commandment. It was a matter of when and how. The when would be immediately, and the how would be as soon as I figured out what it meant to leave the New Age and be a Christian. I'd lived under deception for fifty-eight years! What did it look like to trust God for everything? How was it possible to lean on God instead of trying to predict or control my future?

As the vision faded away, all I could do was gulp and think to myself, *People are going to be really mad at me!* And my conclusion was true: some people *did* become really angry about my conversion, as you'll read.

What Does It Mean to Be a Christian?

I'd always been transparent with my audience about my experiences and insights. Since hearing Alistair Begg's "Itching Ears" sermon in January 2015, and reading the Gospels in 2016, I spoke more often and openly about Jesus at my events, on my weekly radio show, and in my writings. People noticed this too. So they probably weren't surprised when I posted a video on January 9, 2017, called "Jesus Healing Light Meditation." I was still in the New Age, thus the New Agey–style title. I pieced together a rough representation of my vision experience, using images I found on the internet.

In the video, I tried to convey the importance of following the true Jesus who is recorded in the Bible. I'm not even sure if I was saved then, because I still hadn't repented. Not that repenting earns you salvation. It's just that repentance is a sign that you're saved. Jesus Himself said, "Repent, for the kingdom of heaven is at hand" (Matthew 4:17).

After salvation, the Holy Spirit loudly convicts you of your sins and you no longer want to sin (John 16:8). I didn't want to sin either at that time, but I was like a tourist trying to drive in a foreign country without knowing the road rules. I had no idea what constituted a sin and what didn't.

I told a few people at church about the vision. They all thought it was great but didn't offer much advice. My pastor suggested that I make appointments to see a spiritual director, which is like a Christian life coach. I did, and while I enjoyed our sessions, she still didn't advise me of how to change my life and get out of the New Age. She said that I could stay exactly as I was, using angel cards and crystals for healing, while pointing to her own collection of crystals on her shelf.

The Bible discusses crystals throughout the Old and New Testaments. The Levite priests even wore crystals on their ephods (linen chest coverings). The Urim and Thummim appear to have been crystal. Yet there's a big difference between admiring God's gorgeous gemstone creations and using them as idols. In the New Age, we believed that crystals would amplify our healing energy, just as crystals are used in electronics. New Agers also ascribe healing and divination properties to each type of crystal. For example, a rose quartz crystal is said to help you open your heart to romantic love. A clear quartz crystal is said to boost your psychic abilities, and so forth.

Yes, some will argue, but didn't the high priests use the Urim and Thummim crystals for divination to get guidance and answers? Theologians say there's not enough information in the Bible to know exactly how the Urim and Thummim were used, whether it was similar to casting lots, or whether God appeared through them as He did with the ark of the covenant. One thing's clear about the Urim and Thummim, though: God directed their creation and use (Exodus 28:30). It wasn't like the high priest thought up the idea and then found some crystals and designated them as Urim and Thummim. The whole process was God directed.[4] Be careful about people inventing or "channeling" unbiblical and unsubstantiated theories about the Urim and Thummim.

The bottom line is that we are called and commanded to turn to God, and God alone, for answers (Proverbs 3:5–6). We're also told to worship and serve the Creator, not His creation (Romans 1:25). We must be very honest with ourselves and the Holy Spirit about our intentions for having or using crystals. Are they decorations? Or are they viewed as having some curative property?

I also have a personal request for Christian women to be aware that some crystal necklaces are symbols that you are a New Ager. A Google image search of "New Age crystal necklaces" will show which types of necklace fall in this category. Primarily, this includes crystal-point pendants or earrings (crystal points are used as pendulums for divination and psychic protection). Wearing these New Age–inspired necklaces could unwittingly cause unbelievers and baby Christians to stumble, because they imply that it's okay to blend New Age and Christianity. In the appendix, I've included a list of reasons why they can't blend.

During this time of confusion about how to leave the New Age and live as a Christian, I somehow found a book called *The Light That Was Dark* by Warren B. Smith and read it in one night.[5] It was the story of Smith's immersion in Eastern New Age practices of meditation. Smith and his wife, Joy, then got involved with groups studying *A Course in Miracles*, the "Jesus-channeled" New Age bible that I mentioned earlier.

Warren and Joy had lived in the same county as my parents: Butte County, California, which is now famous for the horrible "camp fire" of November 2018, which burned everything to the ground. My parents had sold their Magalia home and moved in with Michael and me one year before the fire burned their house. Anyway, the point is that Warren and Joy Smith and my mother knew many of the same people.

My mom originally introduced me to *A Course in Miracles* by gifting me with Marianne Williamson's book on the topic *A Return to Love.* My mom also used to attend *Course* study groups in Magalia with some of Warren and Joy's friends.

The Light That Was Dark is a well-written autobiography of Warren and Joy's spiritual journey into darkness and how Jesus saved them. Without spoiling the ending of their story—as I highly recommend that you read their book—let me just say that they provided stark comparisons between what Scripture says and what *A Course in Miracles* says. This side-by-side comparison showed that *Course* is the opposite of the Bible!

Since my January 7, 2017, epiphany about the Bible's inerrancy, I'd been reading Scripture daily. My son Grant had gifted me with *The One Year Bible*, New Living Translation, which prompts you to daily read a passage from the Old and New Testaments, plus a psalm and a proverb.[6] In a year, you've read the whole Bible.

Still, I didn't quite understand what I was reading. The Holy Spirit was using Scripture to mold and shape me, and it was working! I was hungry to read the Bible, like a starving woman who hadn't eaten a full meal her whole life.

Reading *The Light That Was Dark* impressed me with the importance of comparing everything to Scripture. Sometime later, I started watching and made a guest appearance on a YouTube show called *Fighting for the Faith* with Pastor Chris Rosebrough, who also compared Scripture against what popular preachers were saying. Watching Pastor Rosebrough convinced me to stop following some false teachers whom I'd assumed were solid Christians when I was first saved.

After reading *The Light That Was Dark*, I threw away all my copies of *A Course in Miracles.* I'd always been a truth seeker, and I knew in my soul that the Bible was the truth. Into the trash went my expensive collector's copies of *A Course in Miracles,* along with its concordance and commentaries. Amazingly, instead of grieving over the wasted time and money invested in *Course,* I felt a big weight lift from me as I threw these items away.

I later wrote and introduced myself to Warren and Joy Smith, and we developed a friendship that continues to this day. As ex–New Agers themselves, the Smiths have lovingly helped me navigate out of deception and into the *true* light of Jesus.

TEN

Tossing the Idols

After noticing how great I felt once the copies of *A Course in Miracles* were in the trash, I was encouraged to keep going. I carried a large, sturdy trash bag and walked through my home, while praying for the Holy Spirit to reveal what I needed to discard. I filled several bags with New Age and occult books, statues of pagan deities, crystals used for New Age purposes, artwork of goddesses, and jewelry, clothing, and yoga mats with New Age symbols. Into the trash bag they all went.

These items can be gateways for demons and spiritual warfare. Demons could be attracted to any item used to conjure, manifest, predict, divine, or manipulate "the energies" or "the universe" or make contact with goddesses or other deities. You don't want to have any item that the demons perceive as an invitation for their presence. New Age items look like welcome mats to demons.

In Acts 19:19, we read about a large bonfire that new Christians had, burning their sorcery books and amulets. They most likely burned these items to ensure the items didn't end up in someone else's hands and lead to further deception. Burning, destroying, or throwing them away may help prevent other people from being deceived.

The reason is that these items had become idols, and I was worshiping them by believing they had the power to heal, manifest, amplify prayers, and so forth. The deity statues also violated God's second commandment: "You shall not make for yourself a carved image, or any likeness of anything that is in heaven above, or that is in the earth beneath, or that is in the water under the earth" (Exodus 20:4). In other words, don't worship statues, paintings, carvings, or such. My home had been filled with statues and paintings of Buddhas, Quan Yin (a female Buddhist "goddess of compassion"), various Hindu deities, angels, Jesus, and Mother Mary. I mistakenly believed these idols would help me, until the Bible and Warren Smith's book showed me they'd actually hurt me.

Some people say it's fine to have Jesus statues or paintings in your home, unless you find yourself "worshiping" the object or if the Holy Spirit personally convicts you about the object. I'm going to admit something embarrassing to you, in case it's helpful to someone else: whenever I saw the Jesus paintings in my home, I found myself thinking or saying a greeting of, "Hi Jesus!" to the painting. I'd catch myself doing this, even though I intellectually realized the painting wasn't really Jesus. After all, the Bible really doesn't tell us much about Jesus' physical appearance. Still, I kept mentally greeting Jesus through these paintings, and the Holy Spirit personally convicted me that I was violating the second commandment of "no graven images" (Exodus 20:4 KJV).

So I also threw away my images of Jesus, including the decks of Jesus cards I'd previously made. The fact that the process of throwing away Jesus art felt so painful told me that I really had made those paintings and statues into idols. Jesus is my Lord and Savior, and I want to obey Him by doing my best to adhere to the moral law (the Ten Commandments) that we Christians are still under. This is not legalism, which is defined as believing you are saved by your works. This is adherence to Jesus' statement, "If you love me, you will keep my commandments" (John 14:15). Once we are saved, we *want* to please and obey God.

Occultic and New Age objects can attract demons and increase the experience of spiritual warfare activity in your home. This is what happened to me when I was first saved. Up until that time, the demons had masqueraded as angels of light. So they "played nice" because I was unknowingly cooperating with their evil scheme of deception.

But when I was saved and my eyes were opened to the truth, I stopped cooperating with these fallen angels. So they began punishing me and showing their true evil colors. Their angry presence was palpable, as if some invisible force was pushing against me. I later connected this experience to Isaiah 61:3 (KJV) as "the spirit of heaviness," which is lifted by putting on the garment of praise (praising God sincerely for His attributes).

Got Questions Ministries explained it this way:

> Occult practices may attract evil spirits, and, since certain objects are used in those practices, it might seem that the demons are attracted to the objects; however, this does not mean the demons are in the objects. It is the occult activity itself that attracts them. When people who have been involved in the occult come to Christ, they are often advised to get rid of their occult books and objects, not because the objects have demons in them, but because the books and objects would be a source for future temptation.[1]

In his book *The Second Coming of the New Age*, ex–New Ager Steven Bancarz discusses how he burned his New Age and occultic possessions. Bancarz recalled, "In my experience, these types of materials kept an extra set of blinders on me after I came to Christ. They stunted me from being able to walk in complete spiritual victory because my soul was still constantly associated with occult objects that surrounded me." Just as I'd experienced, Bancarz said that after he disposed of these items, he noticed more peace and mental clarity and a reduction in spiritual warfare in his home.[2]

I've received letters from ex–New Agers who are tempted back into deception because they have held on to cards or metaphysical books. This is like an alcoholic keeping whiskey or beer in his or her home. We need to remove temptations, especially since demons are attracted to these objects.

So when I went around my home and office with the trash bag, praying for the Holy Spirit to show me which items to dispose of, I never once considered selling or donating the items, even though I'd invested so much money in them. After all, I didn't want to cause another person to stumble into deception.

Some people burn these items to ensure no one else can use them, and other people smash the items. Those are both good actions, if it's practical. At the time, I lived on the ranch, and burning objects could have been a fire hazard. So I threw the items in the trash.

Here are the items I threw away:

- Books from New Age, metaphysical, self-help, and occult authors. Any unbiblical publications.
- Cards used for divination. That included the cards I'd made.
- Clothing with New Age symbols, Sanskrit (such as the Om symbol), or pagan deity images on them.
- Crystals used for divination and New Age methods of healing.
- Dream catchers.
- Jewelry with New Age symbols (such as "sacred geometry") and crystal point pendants, which are symbols of the New Age movement.
- Statues of pagan deities, fairies, angels, and so on. Some of these made of porcelain or ceramic, I was able to smash. The second commandment forbids us to worship graven images.

- Wands made of crystal, used for "manifesting" because they supposedly increased power.
- New Age, occult music, and Eastern meditation CDs and electronic recordings.
- DVDs of New Age movies.
- Essential oil blends that were marketed as New Age tools to clear chakras, communicate with angels, and so forth. I kept the essential oils that I use for cleaning and fragrance, since they aren't used in idolatrous ways.
- I also deleted New Age and occultic apps from my mobile devices.

The Golden Calf

It was an emotional experience throwing these objects away. I'd collected them throughout the years, and they represented memories and experiences. Hardest of all was throwing away my own books and cards, as I'd forsaken time with family and friends to write them. I once believed that those publications were contributions I was making on behalf of God. I was so deceived!

It was also difficult to toss out the expensive gold and gemstone necklaces, bracelets, and crystal wands that had cost a small fortune to purchase. They were also beautiful items, but they represented something extremely ugly. Just as the Bible shows that Satan was a beautiful (Ezekiel 28:11–19) and proud (Isaiah 14:12–14) angel, his pride and ambition cast him out of heaven.

Yet, it was even more of a relief to throw these items away. Each time I placed an item in the trash bag, I could feel a weight lift from my chest and shoulders. The heavier the trash bag became, the lighter I felt.

Our home seemed more peaceful too. When I was first saved and the spiritual warfare was at its height, I struggled with insomnia. It was like the demons were bumping into me and yanking on my blankets all night, and my mind buzzed with random racing thoughts. I resorted to taking melatonin tablets to sleep and still experienced anxiety and sleeplessness.

As I threw away the New Age items, I was able to reduce my melatonin dosages and get some sleep. After we moved away from the ranch, I still took melatonin to sleep. Then one day I found a box in the garage of our new home that had been shipped from the ranch.

The box contained a few of my old books and a two-foot long crystal wand that was encased in gold and gemstones. I'd had this wand custom-made by a woman who called herself an alchemist, around 2004 or 2005, and it had cost $5,000. Several years earlier, the wand had gone missing. I'd assumed that someone had borrowed it from my home and didn't return it. Yet, here was the wand in our new home.

I didn't hesitate for even a moment before throwing that wand in the trash. The crystal was encased in metal, so it would have been difficult to smash. I just wanted that item out of the house! That night, I finally slept without melatonin and I haven't needed to take sleep supplements since.

The golden calf incident is an iconic example of idolatry in the Bible, and the phrase "golden calf" can be a synonym for an idol. Through examining this passage, we can glean insights into the factors that lead humans to rebel against God's commandments, which forbid idolatry. Indeed, we can gain a deeper understanding about the character and nature of God as we examine why He commands us not to worship idols.

Most people would probably describe their personal idols as tamer than the golden calf incident, and rationalize that they're not worshiping a statue. However, the definition of an idol worship is broader than bowing before a statue. As biblical Greek scholar Bill Mounce wrote, "Idolatry is not limited to the worship of false images, but it is placing anything or anyone before God as the object of allegiance and devotion."[3] J. A. Motyer defines an idol as "whatever your heart clings to or relies on for ultimate security. The idol is whatever claims the loyalty that belongs to God alone."[4]

One of the meanings of the Hebrew word *idol* is "worthless," used in the context that any god but the Lord is worthless. Mounce said the root word of *idol* may be "to be weak or deficient." He emphasized this point in view of Psalm 96:5: "In contrast to the omnipotence of the Lord, other gods are weak. The Lord created the heavens, while all the gods of other nations are worthless idols."[5] God knows that we need Him and that only He can help us. In addition, our life's purpose is to bring glory to God, not to other gods (1 Corinthians 10:31).

Those in false religions are encouraged to worship or "venerate" gods, including polytheistic deities in Eastern sects; ancestors, saints, and archangels in Catholicism; trees and nature spirits in pantheistic systems such as Wicca; and "spirit guides" in New Age systems. Idolatry takes materialistic forms that cross religious divides, such as self-worship and being obsessed with material gain, career advancement, and finances. As Pastor Brad Bigney wrote, "Idolatry is at the center of why we sin. . . . It infiltrates and takes over the heart—the nerve center—determining the way we sin, when we sin, with whom we sin."[6]

While many theologians consider the golden calf incident to be Israel's first act of idolatry, author and Wheaton New Testament Professor G. K. Beale contended that idolatry began in the garden at the moment when Adam replaced his reverence for God with a desire for his new object of worship. Beale said that if we define idolatry as worshiping anything other than God, then we can see in Genesis 3 that "Adam's allegiance shifted from God to himself and probably also to Satan," whose temptation Adam obeys.[7]

My point is that I followed the Holy Spirit's directives and threw away everything connected to my New Age days (basically my whole life). I threw away several thousands of dollars of items that I'd collected during the decades. I knew for a fact that I was done with the New Age and I'd never again read or use those items.

As time went on, the Holy Spirit revealed other idols that I was unknowingly prioritizing above God, such as the approval of people and the desire for physical comfort. Galatians 1:10 helped me to overcome my people-pleasing tendencies: "For am I now seeking the approval of man, or of God? Or am I trying to please man? If I were still trying to please man, I would not be a servant of Christ." Remembering that our Lord Jesus had nowhere to lay His head during His earthly ministry (Matthew 8:20) reminded me that my desire for physical comfort could be an idolatrous stumbling block for me. Reading these Bible verses, and praying for the Holy Spirit to sanctify me and give me strength, has been a real help in overcoming idols.

ELEVEN

Sanctification in the Public Eye

My old friends from the New Age were understandably shaken by my conversion, especially since I was vocally denouncing the New Age. Right after my January 7, 2017, vision of Jesus, I knew that I needed to leave the New Age. But after a lifetime under the deception of Christian Science, *A Course in Miracles*, and the New Age, my thought processes were still deceived.

I'd made YouTube videos since 2009, initially to make predictions for the week to come, based on my choosing three divination cards. These videos were popular, usually having 180,000 views per week.

After my Jesus experience, I began reading the Bible in my videos. As a brand-new baby Christian, my theology was off. I was still unknowingly blending Christianity with New Age beliefs. For example, it was extremely difficult for me to say the words *sin, devil, hell,* and *evil.* In my videos, I used the New Age euphemistic term *lower energies* instead.

My old videos also said that Jesus wasn't judging anyone and neither was I. I was unknowingly twisting John 12:47 and trying to walk the middle ground of not offending anyone, which is impossible because the gospel is inherently offensive to those who don't want to admit they're a sinner in need of a Savior. That was before I studied the four Gospels in their entirety and saw that Jesus modeled righteous judgment, which means judging ungodly behavior. When you love God, you hate what God hates, and God hates sin (Psalm 5:5–6; Proverbs 6:16–19; Romans 12:9–10; Jude 23).

I've deleted those old videos, as I don't want anyone to be deceptively influenced by my old beliefs. Some people continue to post my old videos on YouTube to make fun of me, but I can't control that. All I can do is warn people to please study the entire Bible, so they won't be deceived.

As a baby Christian in the public eye, I wanted to do the right thing. Some of my new Christian friends advised me to stay off of social media for a few years, akin to how the apostle Paul went to Arabia for three years after his conversion. My heart was in the right place of wanting to get out of the New Age and follow Jesus, but I was frightened of offending people, of losing New Age family and friends, and of losing income that we needed to support the people and animals in our care.

As I mentioned earlier, I had sessions with a spiritual director. As I sat in her living room, explaining my background, she shared that she was a female Episcopal priest (ordained women are called priests in the Episcopal Church) presiding over a small congregation. This was before discarding my New Age materials. I showed her my decks of cards and explained my fears and confusion about changing my life.

She reassured me that I didn't need to change anything in terms of deleting cards or crystals from my lifestyle. I simply needed to add Jesus and the Bible, and she said that I should embrace my gifts from God.

I should've felt elated at her counsel that I didn't need to change much, but my stomach tightened at her words. I felt a cautionary warning within me, but as a biblically illiterate person, I didn't know *why* her words upset me instead of reassuring me. So I kept seeing her for a few more months.

Now I realize the Holy Spirit was convicting me against following her counsel. The upset I felt was *conviction* from the Holy Spirit, who steers saved people away from sin and back to God's will. I almost fell for her advice since she seemed wiser and more biblically educated than I was. Ultimately though, it was the author of the Bible—the Holy Spirit—who taught me what was right.

This experience taught me the importance of researching spiritual directors and Christian life coaches before engaging their services. Just because someone is certified in these capacities does not mean he or she teaches in biblically correct ways. Before hiring a spiritual director or life coach, please ask him or her the following question: "Do you believe the Bible is God's inerrant Word?" You may feel intrusive asking this question, but trust me, the answer is important. People who believe the Bible is "sort of" true will give you half-truths. Those who think the Bible is a suggestion will give you unbiblical suggestions.

Ask the spiritual director or life coach who he or she believes Jesus is. If the person tells you that Jesus is "just a man" who was a wonderful role model and teacher, please don't book an appointment with that person. You only want to work with professionals who believe the Bible is God's inerrent Word (2 Timothy 3:16–17) and who know that Jesus is the second person of the Holy Trinity.

Even if they profess to believe in Jesus and the Bible, continue to compare their advice to Scripture. After we moved from Hawaii to the Pacific Northwest, I engaged a second spiritual director, who advised me to engage in "contemplative prayer," which as I discuss in this book can be spiritually dangerous and leave us open to demonic deception. Fortunately, by that time, I knew enough about the Bible to discontinue our sessions.

As biblical counselor Mark Baker wrote:

One powerful scheme of deception is to package something that *sounds* good, *feels* good, *seems* good [Proverbs 14:12] or is good, with a lie. Instead of detecting the overall deceit, many Christians will argue for and defend falsehoods and false teachers. They do so for one common reason: "Yeah but, there is some good in that," or "Yeah but, it works!" or "Yeah but, it's helpful . . . useful . . . has some value . . . I felt so close to God . . ." etc. Countless deceptions have occurred, and an untold number of lives damaged or destroyed, by the *yeah-but-there's-some-good* subtle fallacy.

Baker compares this temptation to accept lies-mixed-with-truth, with Eve in the garden.[1] I certainly was guilty of that at first. For instance, I was using a system called "bibliomancy," in which you pray for guidance, close your eyes, and open the Bible to the first page that opens for you. This seemed like a safer alternative than using cards. Then I realized this was a dangerous system, too, as what would happen if I landed on the words from Judas of Iscariot, one of Job's misguided friends, or even Satan's words from Genesis or Jesus' temptation? It was still divination, which God forbids (Deuteronomy 18:10–12). So I stopped using that system too.

Meanwhile, several Christians debated online whether or not my salvation was genuine. I was still confused and trying to figure out what constituted Christian behavior versus New Age behavior. My thoughts were still New Age, such as automatically looking for meanings and omens in number patterns and astrology. I'd repent and give those thoughts to God each time.

I still had two workshops that I'd contracted to give, and I prayed about how to speak to a New Age audience as a Christian. I realized that talking about Jesus and salvation would offend some audience members and that people would complain and ask for refunds because my talk would differ from their expectations. Still, I viewed these workshops as opportunities to share the gospel with New Agers. Social media tongues wagged that I was speaking at New Age workshops, so I must not be saved. It wasn't easy to go through those experiences of giving Christian talks at New Age seminars, and I was thankful for the letters I received afterward from people who *heard* the gospel messages I gave. All glory to God, I was able to plant seeds for His kingdom.

I felt like someone who'd moved to a foreign country and didn't yet speak the language. Even though I'd been listening to Christian radio for fifteen years and attending Christian churches intermittently with apostate churches (Unity, Christian Science, and Religious Science), there were jargon phrases and words that Christians spoke with which I was unfamiliar. Christians said "for a season" instead of "for a while," and "let's camp on [or "unpack"] this verse," instead of, "let's study this verse." It was like learning a whole new language while deleting my old language. I had to stop saying *vibes, energies, ego,* and other New Age terms. Even more important, I needed to stop thinking like a New Ager.

Little did I realize in those early stages that I was being sanctified, which is a purification process that God conducts on believers throughout their earthly lives. In the New Age, I believed that I was in charge of my thoughts. In the sanctification process, I learned to trust that Jesus was in charge.

Baptism

I'd never been baptized, as the Christian Science church where I was raised doesn't ascribe to water baptism in the name of the Holy Trinity. Throughout my life, it had never occurred to me to get baptized.

My brother Ken had been baptized twenty years earlier when he converted to Christianity. At that time, I'd seen photos of him in a baptism robe at his church's baptismal pool, but it didn't seem to have anything to do with my life. I just thought that Ken and his Christian wife, Jann, were taking a more traditional route than I was. Sometimes I even blamed Jann for influencing my brother away from our family's New Age beliefs. I've since repented and apologized to Jann for holding that false judgment about her. That experience also helps me to deal with people who accuse my husband, Michael, of converting me to Christianity. It wasn't Michael's idea—it was all God's good work in saving us both.

Soon after my vision of Jesus, I couldn't wait to be baptized and I was hungry to read the entire Bible. My baptism was planned for February 25, 2017. I had to take preparatory classes to understand the meaning and commitment of baptism. We aren't saved by baptism, but baptism is an outward symbol of our commitment to Jesus, much like a marriage ceremony. Baptism is symbolic of dying and resurrecting with Christ, and the cleansing and the new heart that we receive at salvation (Mark 16:16; Acts 2:38; Romans 6:3–4).

I was set to be baptized by full immersion in the ocean cove near Kawaihae Harbor, north of Kona, Hawaii. Usually, this cove was calm, but the day of my baptism was stormy with big ocean swells. The pastor and my husband, Michael, walked me out past the surf break and stood on either side of me to keep the waves from knocking me down. A friend from church kindly offered to sit on a nearby seawall, playing "Awesome God" by Rich Mullins on her ukulele during the baptism.

I spoke aloud my commitment to follow Jesus as my Lord and Savior and renounce the devil. Then, I held my nose and mouth closed to avoid inhaling sea water as Michael and Pastor David held me securely and dunked me completely underwater in the name of the Father, the Son, and the Holy Ghost. I actually felt like some evil being was evicted from me during the baptism. The process was the closest thing I could imagine to an exorcism. In the New Age, we would've called this experience a "deep spiritual detox."

As I walked to the beach, wearing a now heavily water-soaked dress, I was hugged by family members, including my stepdaughter,

Ashley; my mother (who is still a Christian Scientist as of the publication of this book; please pray for her); Sharry, the mother of my daughter-in-law Melissa; and Sharry's partner, Roger, who took photos and videos of the baptism. The ceremony was a sweet celebration of my new life in Christ, even though I still didn't completely understand what that meant.

Bible Reading

I started reading *The One Year Bible* that my son Grant had sent me as a gift. The New Living Translation (NLT) was so much easier for my baby Christian mind to comprehend, compared to the King James Version (KJV) I'd grown up with and its Old English grammar. It was mid-March when I started reading the page marked January 1, and I never did catch up so that the calendar day on *The One Year Bible* matched the date I was reading it. Sometimes I'd get obsessive compulsive about this discrepancy, but it wasn't a discouragement or distraction.

I loved reading the Bible! What a difference in reading it after salvation. Before that time, I'd tried reading the entire Bible and would always stop after getting to Exodus or Leviticus. The Bible says that "the message of the cross is foolishness to those who are perishing, but to us who are being saved it is the power of God" (1 Corinthians 1:18 NKJV). In other words, the gospel makes no sense unless we are being saved. The gospel is veiled (hidden) to those who are perishing. The devil has blinded the minds of unbelievers so they cannot see the light of the gospel of the glory of Christ, who is the image of God (2 Corinthians 4:3–4).

Jesus described this sad phenomenon in the parable of the sower, which is a story illustrating how the devil tries to keep us from following Jesus. In this parable, Jesus discussed a gardener sowing seeds on four different types of surfaces: (1) the road; (2) rocky places; (3) thorny places; and (4) good soil. As would be expected, the seeds only grew in the good soil. Jesus explained what the seeds thrown on the road represented: "When anyone hears the word of the kingdom and does not understand it, the evil one (the devil) comes and snatches away what has been sown in his heart" (Matthew 13:19).

When Jesus saves us and we commit to following Him, the Holy Spirit enters us. Our spiritual blindness is lifted, and we can understand the Bible. The apostle Paul explained that we must have the Holy Spirit within us in order to understand the Bible: "The person without the Spirit does not accept the things that come from the Spirit of God but considers them foolishness, and cannot understand them because they are discerned only through the Spirit" (1 Corinthians 2:14 NIV).

No wonder I couldn't understand the Bible before I was saved! I didn't have the Holy Spirit dwelling within me. After all, the Holy Spirit wrote the Bible through forty-plus human authors. The reason why the Bible is so consistent from Genesis 1:1 to Revelation 22:21 is because the same Spirit wrote through each author. When we are saved by Jesus, the Holy Spirit dwells within us as our Comforter, Advocate, and Teacher (Isaiah 11:2; John 14:16, 26; 16:13; 1 Corinthians 2:13). As our teacher and the author of the Bible (2 Peter 1:21), the Holy Spirit helps us understand the Bible and tuck verses into our hearts.

Before I was saved, I'd stopped reading the Bible because I couldn't understand why it contained violence, animal sacrifices, rape, incest, and other troubling scenarios. After salvation, I saw that the Bible is a historical account of the depravity and sinful behaviors of humanity when we turn away from God. The book of Judges is a horrifying account of a time when people did whatever they wanted and the resulting anarchy because they stopped obeying God. As you read the Bible, you realize that God condemns these sinful behaviors. In other words, the fact that the Bible talks about rape or incest does not mean that God condones these sinful, hurtful actions. It's actually the opposite, as reading the Bible reveals.

The Bible is the most amazing story ever told, and it's important to read it from beginning to end to see the big picture. That way we can see how God enacted His plan of redeeming sinful humanity in Genesis 3:15, and how God patiently and mercifully shepherds His people who continually turn toward idols. In the Old Testament, God spoke through His appointed prophets to warn people of the consequences for disobedience and to promise a future Savior, who appeared as Jesus, fully God and fully human.

The Old Testament showed the sacrificial system to atone for sins by slaying unblemished lambs. These sacrifices had to be continually repeated because they didn't have the lasting power to cleanse humanity. That's why God sent His only begotten Son, the second person of the Trinity, to earth to be the perfect, unblemished lamb sacrifice for all time. After Jesus' death on the cross, the temple curtain tore to the holy of holies, which had previously been only available to high priests to meet with God once a year. Through Jesus' willingness to be sacrificed for our sins, believers have direct access to speak with God. Jesus was raised from the dead after three days, and He now sits at the right hand of the Father.

All the prophecies about the coming Messiah that we read in the Old Testament were fulfilled in the person of Jesus Christ. There are so many layers to the Bible that you could study it for a lifetime and still find more.

I noticed that I was thinking about the Bible throughout the day. I'd be cleaning the house, while thinking of how Joseph coped with his time in Egypt by trusting in God, or a proverb would pop into my mind. I also noticed that when I saw social media posts of Scripture, my heart raced like a teenager in love. I was tucking Scripture into my heart and falling in love with God's Word.

Queen Esther

I also loved reading about the strong women in the Bible, such as Queen Esther. The book of Esther is about the Jewish community who remained living in Susa, the capital city of the Persian Empire under King Xerxes, after some of the Israelites returned to Jerusalem from exile.

God is never mentioned in the book of Esther, so it's an invitation to read the story and look for God's activity behind the scenes. One message of the book is that when God seems absent and people are unfaithful to the Torah, God is still there, using the faith of even morally compromised people to accomplish His purposes. The book invites us to trust God's promises and His commitment to redeeming His world.[2]

The book of Esther opens with King Xerxes throwing an elaborate banquet to glorify himself and then demanding that his wife display her beauty to his banquet guests. The queen refused and so was deported in the king's drunken rage. He held a beauty pageant to find a replacement queen, and Esther, who hid her Jewish heritage, won. Mordecai, her cousin, overheard a murder plot against the king. Esther relayed this plot to the king, and Mordecai was credited as a hero.

We next meet Haman, a descendant of the Canaanites, whom the king had elevated to a high-level position. Haman represents the self-absorbed (Esther 6:6) and self-indulgent (Esther 3:5–6) pagans where Esther lived.[3] Haman demanded that everyone kneel before him, but Mordecai refused, which enraged Haman. So, Haman persuaded the king to a decree that would destroy Mordecai and all the other Jewish people on a day decided by rolling the dice (dice in Hebrew is *pur*). Esther and Mordecai planned that she would approach the king about this plot and reveal that she was Jewish and, therefore, in peril. However, there was a risk because queens were only allowed to approach kings by appointment. That's when Mordecai uttered the iconic phrase, "And who knows whether you have not attained royalty for such a time as this?" (Esther 4:14 NASB).

King Xerxes then recalled that Mordecai had saved his life, so he ordered Haman to honor Mordecai. The next day, Esther revealed her Jewish heritage and Haman's plot to kill her and other Jews. The king ordered Haman's death, and he allowed the Jews to defend themselves on the day that Haman had plotted. This event is commemorated with an annual two-day feast called Purim, named after the *pur* (dice) that were thrown.[4]

Bible Commentaries

In addition to reading the Bible, I like to read theological commentaries to help me understand the context and original biblical language meanings. Several commentators liken Esther to Joseph, who was sold into slavery and then elevated to an Egyptian leader. Just as Joseph concluded that his painful condition was meant for evil but God ultimately used it for good (Genesis 50:20), so did Mordecai reassure Esther that she had been born for such a time as this (Esther 4:14). These reminders that God can use all things for good (Romans 8:28) can lend hope that good will come out of a season of struggle.

As I grieved over my sinful years of teaching New Age deception, and influencing people away from the Bible, I took comfort in the story of Esther. I prayed that God could use my New Age past for His glory.

The book of Ruth became another favorite that inspired and encouraged me. The main idea of the book of Ruth is how two widows, a mother-in-law and a daughter-in-law, survived the loss of their husbands and their long journey to Bethlehem, where God provided for their needs. A lot is packed into this relatively short (four-chapter) book. Ruth met and married her redeemer, Boaz, and they had a son who was an ancestor of Jesus' lineage.

We can apply the themes of Ruth to our lives today, especially for those who are trying to earn salvation by their own works. Ruth's gracious willingness to be saved by Boaz paints a beautiful picture of our need to surrender to God's will. We need to acknowledge our need to be saved by Jesus. This was a big revelation for me, as I was fiercely independent. It took time and prayer to learn how to wait on the Lord and submit my will to His. I now trust that He knows better than I do.

Despite the growth of my personal convictions and theological understanding, though, I continued to use oracle cards in my weekly videos. I was struggling with people-pleasing fears of disappointing my video audience, who tuned in to see the card readings. I also didn't want to disappoint my publisher, who was nervously on edge from my conversion. I'm not blaming others for my sinful actions; I'm explaining the underlying fears in case someone reading this can relate to these feelings and actions.

TWELVE

Repentance

Every answer I'd been seeking was in the Bible, and it had been on my bookshelf my entire life, patiently waiting for me to open and read it. Finally, I was learning in definitive and trustworthy Scripture about the meaning of life, God's purpose for me, the afterlife, and other questions I'd had since adolescence.

Then—and this part of my testimony is really big!—when I read Deuteronomy 18, the pieces of my conversion and salvation came together. I *finally* got it through my thick, stubborn head that *I am a sinner who needs a Savior* when I read this: "There shall not be found among you anyone who burns his son or his daughter as an offering, anyone who practices divination or tells fortunes or interprets omens, or a sorcerer" (v. 10).

The backstory context of this passage is that God was speaking through Moses, who had been leading the Israelites out of Egyptian slavery, through the wilderness, and into the promised land. The pagan Canaanites were then living in the promised land, and they were about to be ousted because of their paganism. God was warning the Israelites not to practice the pagan ways of the Canaanites they would meet in the promised land, or they, too, would be exiled from the promised land. In the verse preceding this passage, God said through Moses: "When you come into the land that the LORD your God is giving you, you shall not learn to follow the abominable practices of those nations" (Deuteronomy 18:9).

Deuteronomy 18:10 refers to the pagan practices of the Canaanites, who threw their infant babies into burning incinerators within the statues of their pagan deity Molech. The Canaanites believed that infant sacrifice would earn them blessings from Molech. In this verse, God was forbidding the Israelites from engaging in this horrendous practice. Most of us today would say that we'd never engage in such actions.

But there's more: the second part of verse 10 puts the practice of divination, fortune-telling, interpreting omens, and sorcery in the same horrible category as sacrificing a baby to a pagan deity! That means that divination and fortune-telling (using cards, horoscopes, astrology, rune stones, palm and tea leaf reading; crystal balls and scrying; and so forth) are equal to child sacrifice in God's eyes.

I choked up and my knees buckled as I read this list of sinful activities, for I had engaged in divination and fortune-telling for years! I'd mistakenly believed that these activities were helping people and, therefore, helping God. What deception had blinded me! How could I help people if I was conducting sinful activities like divination and mediumship? I definitely wasn't helping God with these New Age practices, as I'd previously imagined. Besides, God doesn't need humanity's help; it's we humans who need God's help.

Then there's the part in verse 10 about interpreting omens. This refers to looking for signs and omens, such as reading meaning into songs, thoughts, birds, and other naturally occurring experiences and objects. Well, I'd not only engaged in interpreting omens for years, but I'd also written and taught about it. We'd look for feathers, imagining that they had fallen from angel wings, and then we'd interpret these feathers to mean whatever desire we wanted to validate.

In Deuteronomy 18, we continue reading about the pagan practices of the Canaanites whom God was commanding the Israelites to avoid: "or a charmer or a medium or a necromancer or one who inquires of the dead" (v. 11).

I'm so ashamed to admit this now, but I used to conduct, teach, and write about mediumship. I thought that getting messages from departed loved ones was a helpful way for people to heal from grief. My intentions were good, and never in a million years did I realize that demons were pretending to be departed loved ones. The messages in these mediumship sessions were comforting and accurate, so I thought they were genuinely from people's friends and family in heaven. I thought of my departed grandparents as my angels, and I believed they sent me signs and help from heaven. But that's mediumship, and the Bible said that God found people who practiced this to be abominations and detestable.

One of the reasons why God prohibits mediumship may be because He's protecting us from demonic deception. The story of King Saul and the witch of En-dor in 1 Samuel 28 illustrates the spiritual deception of demons pretending to be departed people during mediumship sessions. Saul was desperate to receive guidance from the prophet Samuel, who'd recently passed away. Even though Saul had banished mediums from Israel, he went to see the witch of En-dor late one night to see if she could conjure Samuel. The Hebrew language of this biblical passage uses similar words as given in the prohibitions against mediumship in Leviticus 19:31 and 20:27 and Deuteronomy 18:10–11.

When the witch of En-dor began her mediumship session with Saul, she told him, "I see *elohim* ['gods'] coming up from the earth," using *elohim* with a plural verb. Theologian G. J. R. Kent said this biblical grammar is consistent with polytheism, which is the worship of deities other than God. Saul believed he was talking with the prophet Samuel during the session, who predicted the death of Saul and his sons.

Kent noted that if it were the *real* Samuel speaking with Saul, he would've rebuked the king for using divination and mediumship and told him to repent, especially with his death foretold. The fact that this "Samuel" spirit said that Saul would be with him the next day was also an ominous signal that the demon was predicting Saul joining him in the second death. Although Saul died by suicide the next day, the reason for his death was because of his sin of consulting a medium, according to 1 Chronicles 10:13–14. In addition, Samuel's prophecies were always 100 percent accurate, which is a mark of a true prophet. In contrast, the spirit conjured by the witch of En-dor gave an inaccurate prediction of Saul and his sons' deaths. As Kent concluded:

> This dark and murky tale seems intended to make the audience feel and experience the deception of Saul, and to invite careful considera-
> tion of the subtle clues in the text to determine what is really going
> on. . . . Thus the story echoes timeless biblical warnings against
> necromancy [mediumship] as opposed to genuine prophecy.[1]

My worldview was unraveling. All those years, had I been talking with demons posing as angels and departed loved ones? The next verse of Deuteronomy 18 completely broke me: "For whoever does these things is an abomination to the LORD. And because of these abomi-nations the LORD your God is driving them out before you" (v. 12).

What?! You mean that all these New Age healing methods that I'd learned, taught, and practiced were not from God?! The word *abomination* (*detestable* in the NLT translation I was reading) is very strong. God doesn't direct these terms to the *action*, but to the *person* who does the action. Not only was I not helping God with my New Age practices, but I personally was a detestable abomination to Him!

I fell to my knees, weeping and sobbing loudly, "I'm so sorry, God! I didn't know! Please forgive me!" My heart was filled with remorse, sorrow, and terror. I was horrified that I'd not only disappointed God but was detestable in His eyes as well. I was heartbroken and wanted to run away. But where? God could see me no matter where I went.

Through tear-filled eyes, I continued reading Deuteronomy 18:

> You shall be blameless before the LORD your God, for these nations, which you are about to dispossess, listen to fortune-tellers and to diviners. But as for you, the LORD your God has not allowed you to do this. (vv. 13–14)

This passage from Deuteronomy 18 finally helped me understand, and be saved by, the gospel. I'd held on to the Christian Science doctrine that sin was an illusion and that I was a perfect, whole, and complete child of God, made in His image and likeness. I understood that *I couldn't be saved until I realized I was a sinner who needed to be saved!*

While on my knees, crying, apologizing, and pleading with God, my pride and deception were finally broken by God's Word. I prayed for Jesus to be my Lord and Savior and to lead me. Through reading Deuteronomy 18:10–14, I finally realized:

- I had sinned through my New Age practices of divination, omen interpretation, and mediumship.
- As a sinner, I deserved death (Romans 6:23).
- As a sinner, I would be cast into hell for eternal torment.
- I couldn't save myself from this judgment.
- Only Jesus could save me by His willingness to take the punishment I deserved for my sins.
- I needed Jesus as my Savior.
- I couldn't trust myself to lead my life, because I'd obviously made ungodly choices unknowingly in the past.
- I needed to follow Jesus as a sheep following the Good Shepherd.
- As Jesus said, "If you love me, you will obey me" (John 14:15). I needed to obey Jesus.

- I knew I wasn't saved by my own works, but by my faith in Jesus through God's grace and mercy in extending salvation to me (Ephesians 2:8).
- I wouldn't be obedient in order to be saved, but *because* I was saved. I *wanted* to be obedient.

When I pubicly shared the impact this passage had on me, some New Agers told me that this condemnation of New Age and occultic practices was only in the NLT and ESV Bible translations that I read. These New Agers assured me that older Bible translations weren't condemning of pagan practices. So, I checked, but sure enough, the King James Version Bible from the year 1611 said:

> There shall not be found among you any one that maketh his son or his daughter to pass through the fire, or that useth divination, or an observer of times, or an enchanter, or a witch. Or a charmer, or a consulter with familiar spirits, or a wizard, or a necromancer. For all that do these things are an abomination unto the LORD: and because of these abominations the LORD thy God doth drive them out from before thee. (Deuteronomy 18:10–12 KJV)

Every Bible translation I checked gave similar wording (including the Geneva Bible from 1599 and the Wycliffe Bible from 1382). They all said that God detests the people who practice New Age, occultic, and pagan methods. Why? Because God loves us, and He wants us to turn to Him for guidance. God knows that we will receive incorrect guidance if we turn to cards, crystals, pendulums, Ouija boards, mediums, psychics, horoscopes, astrology charts, tea leaves, rune stones, palm reading, and other divination methods. He detests people who use such practices, because we can infect others to follow the same deceptive ways (as I had before Jesus saved me).

Some people argue that Deuteronomy 18 isn't valid today because we're under grace and not law. That's what people say to justify practicing what Deuteronomy prohibits. Yet, Jesus clearly said, "Do not think that I have come to abolish the Law or the Prophets; I have not come to abolish them but to fulfill them" (Matthew 5:17). We are not under the 613 Mosaic ceremonial laws pertaining to sacrifices, mode of dress and eating, but we are still under the Ten Commandments (the "Moral Laws") (Matthew 5:18). Deuteronomy 18 is an explanation of the Ten Commandments.

We also see examples in the New Testament that support the continuation of Deuteronomy 18. For example, as I shared earlier, there's a girl in Acts 16 who was making her managers a lot of money. Why? Because the girl was possessed of a "python spirit" (reminds me of the serpent in Genesis 3), which made her super-psychic. Professor John Byron wrote that the python spirit is a "spirit of divination," referring to the python that originally inhabited the Greek city of Delphi. There, the pagan priestess Pythia would deliver oracles by going into a trance and speaking for the deity Apollo. There seems to be a connection between the Delphi oracle and the fortune-telling that the girl in Acts 16 was performing for her slave owners.[2]

The apostle Paul commanded the python spirit to come out in the name of Jesus Christ, and it left the girl and she was rendered without psychic abilities. Her managers became angry at Paul for the lost revenue (Acts 16:16–24).

We also see New Testament prohibitions against idolatry, witchcraft, and sorcery in Galatians 5:20. Those who practice idolatry or sorcery will also be prohibited from entering the new heaven (Revelation 22:15). Instead, "their portion will be in the lake that burns with fire and sulfur, which is the second death" (Revelation 21:8).

The New Testament clearly condemns Simon the sorcerer, who tried to buy spiritual gifts by giving money to the apostles in exchange for receiving the ability to lay his hands on people and impart the Holy Spirit. The apostle Peter rebuked Simon and said:

"May your money be destroyed with you for thinking God's gift can be bought! You can have no part in this, for your heart is not right with God. Repent of your wickedness and pray to the Lord. Perhaps he will forgive your evil thoughts, for I can see that you are full of bitter jealousy and are held captive by sin."

"Pray to the Lord for me," Simon exclaimed, "that these terrible things you've said won't happen to me!" (Acts 8:20–24 NLT)

That's the last time the Bible speaks about Simon the sorcerer.

It was common for pagan temples to sell their priesthood titles in biblical times, so Simon was likely accustomed to buying his way into religious notoriety.[3] Got Questions Ministries said:

> The greed of Simon is recalled in the modern word *simony*, "using religion as a means of profit." Contemporary Christians should take from the account of Simon that the church, even today, must be careful of those claiming to possess supernatural abilities, and those claiming to be Christians who desire to "buy the gift of God with money," for their "heart is not right before God" (Acts 8:20–21).[4]

I'm ashamed to say that I was similar to Simon the sorcerer in many ways. My life before salvation was a testimony to the ruinous outcome of following a false Christ, a false gospel, and New Age practices. While my career had been successful, my personal life had been a long shamble of failed marriages, and my poor sons had been left behind while I traveled for my career. I'd married unbelievers who had pagan practices and abused drugs and alcohol. I'd divorced instead of fighting and praying for my marriages. I'd followed cards instead of the Bible. I'd followed my feelings instead of God. Now at age fifty-eight I was repenting, learning to lean completely on God, and praying for Him to redeem the damage I'd done from my years of deception.

Judged

Meanwhile, my family, friends, publisher, and event producers were receiving complaints about my conversion. People started to accuse me of being a stereotype of what they imagined a Christian to be like. Before my salvation, I'd held similar judgmental stereotypes about Christians.

My event producer strongly counseled me to only speak about what I was *for* and not to speak about what I was *against*. A family member said I wasn't a true Christian because I was speaking against the false teachings of the New Age, and according to this family member, "Jesus loved and accepted everyone." People sent me letters, urging me to only post the soft and sweet passages of the Bible on social media.

I was still a baby Christian, trying to understand what God wanted for me. If I compromised and offered nonoffensive, feel-good Christianized messages, I could keep my income stream. But at what cost spiritually? I was never one to compromise. Even when I was teaching deception in the New Age, it was the truth to me at that time. I wouldn't write books or give workshops with half-truths about Christianity. I wanted to learn and teach only God's truth.

I was trying to learn from Christian teachers on television, and I almost got caught up in deception again! When I was first saved and still biblically illiterate, I started following a famous female teacher who I assumed was a solid Christian because she held a Bible and quoted from it frequently.

But then I heard her say something that struck me like a punch in the gut. She said that Jesus was born again in hell after He died, and that Jesus was the first person to be born again. Even as a baby Christian, that statement seemed wrong to me. The Holy Spirit was already guiding my theological understanding. So I thankfully found a YouTube program called *Fighting for the Faith* that compared this female teacher's statements to the Bible. Just as I'd suspected, there was nothing in the Bible about Jesus being born again in hell. In fact, just the opposite was true: Jesus didn't need to be born again because He'd never sinned (2 Corinthians 5:21).

I also noticed that she taught that Jesus was a wish granter for material gain, much as Christian Science taught that Jesus was a wish granter for health.

Christian Prophetess

On his *Fighting for the Faith* YouTube channel, Pastor Rosebrough also had videos about *another* female teacher I'd been following who ran a school to become a "certified prophet." After my conversion, I seriously believed that God wanted me to become a Christian prophetess, and I was thinking of going to this school to learn more. Then I watched Pastor Rosebrough's videos and realized that she was teaching exactly what I used to teach in my New Age psychic development classes. Basically, she was teaching to pray and then say whatever popped into your head and heart. I stopped following her at that point, as I didn't want to receive deceptive messages from demons again.

I was still interested in becoming a prophet, and I thought that my spiritual gift might be prophecy, so I continued to research. After all, God is sovereign and can do anything He pleases. I'd learned my lesson, however, and didn't ever again want to be disobedient. I continued to research the qualifications of being a true prophet and reread Deuteronomy 18. When I noticed what God said about the requirements of prophets, I realized that I wasn't qualified to be a prophet. The qualifications to be God's prophet are clearly outlined in the Bible and summarized by R. Douglas Geivett and Holly Pivec in their book *God's Super-Apostles*.[5]

The Fulfillment Test

The Bible says that the prophecies of true prophets are fulfilled 100 percent of the time (Deuteronomy 18:21–22). If even one of your predictions doesn't come true, you're deemed a false prophet. That's because true prophets are mouthpieces for God, and God only speaks the accurate truth of what will happen. While my predictions in the New Age were often accurate, many of the things I predicted didn't come true, so I would've been stoned to death as a false prophet in biblical times.

As Geivett and Pivec remind us:

> When prophets falsely claim to speak for God, they are guilty of breaking God's third commandment: "You shall not take the name of the Lord your God in vain, for the Lord will not hold him guiltless who takes his name in vain" (Exodus 20:7). When many people think of taking God's name in vain, they think only of using his name disrespectfully. But taking God's name in vain also means to use it to deceive someone, as occurs when someone gives a false prophecy.[6]

Some people argue this is an Old Testament rule, as evidenced by the prophet Agabus in the New Testament, who "seemed" in error about his prophecy concerning Paul's arrest. Agabus had prophesied that the Jews would bind Paul and hand him over to the Romans (Acts 21:11). Yet, nowhere in the Bible does it say that Agabus was incorrect; in fact, Paul even retells the story of his arrest using Agabus's own words (Acts 21:30–33; 28:17). Agabus prophesied that the Jews would seize Paul and hand him over to the Gentiles, and that's exactly what occurred. So, prophecy in the New Testament is 100 percent accurate, as in the Old Testament.

The Orthodoxy Test

The orthodoxy test ensures that every prophecy given by a prophet must agree with Scripture. True prophets never contradict or add to

God's Word (Deuteronomy 13:1–5). True prophets also never lead people to worship false gods (Deuteronomy 13:1–3). Much of what I'd taught as a false prophet in the New Age contradicted Scripture, such as teaching the Arianism heresy that Jesus was just a man who was now ascended and helping us as "an ascended master." I also unfortunately led people to idolize angels, the false Jesus, and pagan deities (whom I called "archangels and ascended masters" in the New Age).

As Geivett and Pivec point out, we find the orthodoxy test in the New Testament in 2 Thessalonians 2:1–2 when Paul warned congregants to not be influenced by the false prophecy that contradicted Scripture about the Lord's second coming.

The Lifestyle Test

Jesus said that we can distinguish false from true prophets by their fruit (their actions). The story of the false prophet Bar-Jesus discouraged his friend from hearing and trusting the gospel presentation of the apostle Paul. The false prophet was immediately blinded as a consequence for his sin of preventing a person from hearing the true gospel (Acts 13:5–11).

Geivett and Pivec say that the lifestyle test should be applied to all people proclaiming to be prophets, to see if they are living a godly life, free of sexual immorality, drunkenness, and other sinful behaviors.

Well, I certainly would have flunked the lifestyle test during my New Age years. The hedonistic "follow your bliss" lifestyle would have certainly earned me a false prophet designation. I also had regrettably promoted the New Age as a more "positive" alternative to Christianity. I've repented for all of this, and as a born-again Christian, I'm committed to living a godly lifestyle. We aren't saved by our actions, but our actions show that we are saved.

All this research was pointing me away from trying to be a prophetess at a Christian church. A friend told me that I shouldn't worry about Deuteronomy 18 because that was Old Testament Mosaic law that isn't supported by the New Testament covenant of grace. My friend argued that Jesus only told us to love God and love our neighbors. Back to researching I went!

When Jesus was asked which was the greatest commandment, He said, "You shall love the Lord your God with all your heart and with all your soul and with all your mind. This is the great and first commandment. And a second is like it: You shall love your neighbor as yourself" (Matthew 22:36–39).

Does that mean that all we Christians need to do is love God and people? Well, yes, but notice what Jesus said next: "On these two commandments depend all the Law and the Prophets" (Matthew 22:40). In other words, those two commandments are summaries or umbrellas of all the Law and the Prophets. We are still under the moral law of the Ten Commandments. Jesus said that He came to fulfill, not to abolish the law, including His fulfillment of the fourth commandment as our Sabbath rest.

As theologian Kevin Vanhoozer wrote, the laws outlined by Moses in Deuteronomy 12–26 are based on the content and order of the Ten Commandments.[7] Deuteronomy 18, which forbids divination, mediumship, omen interpretation, witchcraft, and false prophecy is an explanation of the first commandment to worship only God, the second commandment to not worship idols, and the third commandment to not take the Lord's name in vain.

Then I realized that people were following people who were false prophets as I had been, so I started warning others. My prayer is that those who are currently false prophets will fall under the Holy Spirit's conviction as I did, repent, and turn away from delivering messages of false hope, and deliver the full and true good news of the gospel instead.

THIRTEEN

Spiritual Warfare

Meanwhile my family, former publisher, and I received angry social media posts and messages from people who were upset about my conversion. People also made hateful YouTube videos about me. Their accusations included that I was controlled by my husband, Michael; that I was going "backward" in my spirituality because you're "supposed to go from Christianity to New Age, and not the reverse"; that I'd converted in order to make more money in the Christian market; that I'd "ditched the New Agers for the Christians"; that I was under government mind-control operations; and that I was going through a temporary astrological phase called a "Saturn return," whatever that means.

People conjectured that I wasn't really saved. My husband, sons, and daughters-in-law were fielding shockingly hateful letters from people who'd previously told us they stood for "love and light." My former publisher was also inundated by upset customers who wanted to know what was going on with my conversion.

I was experiencing spiritual warfare in awful ways. I'd always been highly sensitive, and I could feel the presence of hatred and anger coming against me. My first thought was, *The witch community is praying against me.* I didn't understand why that would be, as I'd never identified as a witch. But apparently because I'd made a popular deck of cards with goddess images, the witch community took my conversion personally. "Christianity is patriarchal," they kept saying in their angry letters to me, and two or three people validated that witches were indeed casting spells against me and conjuring that I'd return to the New Age. I could feel their anger like daggers and arrows, and I could barely sleep.

In desperation, I researched how to protect oneself from spiritual warfare. Instead of turning to the Bible, which gives complete instructions in Ephesians 6:10–19, James 4:7, and 1 Peter 5:8, I turned to YouTube videos from deliverance ministries, which offer "prayers of protection." These prayers basically command the binding of demons in the name of Jesus. I kept those videos playing around the clock, trying to clear my home of demons. The videos seemed to work, and I had a bit of relief.

But then the oppression would increase. This reminded me of when Jesus described a demon being cast out of a person, and then the demon would gather seven of his demon friends, who were even more evil than he was, and return to the person (Matthew 12:43–45; Luke 11:24–26). So I stopped listening to the deliverance ministry videos.

Pastor Jim Osman, author of *Truth or Territory: A Biblical Approach to Spiritual Warfare,* wrote that, unlike Jesus and the apostles, we are not equipped to rebuke, bind, or cast out demons. Osman points to the biblical passage that says that the archangel Michael would not pronounce judgment against the devil (Jude 8–10).

Osman asks that if not even the archangel Michael will rebuke the devil, how arrogant would it be for us to presume that we can rebuke him? Osman wrote, "Rebuking, commanding, or ridiculing the devil are not tools of effective spiritual warfare; they are marks of prideful, arrogant, self-willed false teachers."

Osman explained that the Bible gives us clear guidelines about dealing with spiritual warfare by resisting the devil (1 Peter 5:9) and standing in the armor of God (Ephesians 6:10–14).[1]

As theologian John M. Frame wrote:

Angels participate in kingdom warfare. Above and around us are good and evil angels, engaged in spiritual warfare. Satan and his hosts engage human beings in the battle by tempting us to sin. The good angels, however, are "ministering spirits sent out to serve for the sake of those who are to inherit salvation" (Hebrews 1:14). The two armies fight one another, as well as fighting against and for us. (Daniel 10:13, 21; Jude 9; Revelation 12:7)[2]

I'd wake up in a cold sweat with my heart racing, feeling as though I was going to die or as if someone was trying to kill me. I could sense nefarious presences in our home, and I felt anxious and tense. My thought was that the devil was angry that I'd left the New Age, so he was out for retribution. I was taking the melatonin supplements to sleep, and as a result I felt drowsy during the day. My mind was foggy, and I also felt tremendous pressure to take a stance and decide: Would I continue to try to blend New Age with Christianity, or would I trust God completely? I felt like someone who needed to jump from a burning building and trust the firefighter to catch me.

Meanwhile, my former publisher reported that my conversion was dramatically affecting my book sales. New Age bookstores were returning my books to the publisher, wanting nothing to do with a Christian author. My former publisher's accountant estimated that my earnings would drop by 70 percent that year, and Michael and I knew it was time to leave Hawaii, with its sky-high costs of living and state tax rates.

My parents lived with us, so we needed to quickly find a home that would give us enough room. My dad specified that he wanted his own garage, and he and my mom wanted two bedrooms and two bathrooms of their own. Michael found a home with an attached mother-in-law home in a Seattle suburb, and he flew out to secure it for us. We had two months to move before the money ran out. At first we tried to sell the ranch, but when that didn't work, we ended up returning the ranch, at a significant financial loss, to the owners from whom we were purchasing it.

We scrambled to find good homes for our farm animals that we couldn't fly to the mainland because of their size and their comfort. These animals had been born and raised in Hawaii, and we couldn't ask them to adjust to the snowy winter where we were moving in November 2017. Besides, we no longer had enough money for their care. We prayed and were able to find homes for all the animals. It was heartbreaking to leave them, as any pet owner can imagine. I still remember the sad way my horse Scout looked at me as I walked him into a trailer and said goodbye as he left for his new home. The grief and the spiritual warfare at that time were breaking any remaining pride I had.

My parents, stepdaughter Ashley, and our dogs and cats flew to Seattle on an overnight flight in November to a home we'd never before visited. We were learning how to lean on God and trust Him with our next steps.

I hung ten different wall plaques that read "Trust in the Lord with all your heart" (Proverbs 3:5) on my office walls at our new home. I needed help in learning how to lean on God. I was so accustomed to "manifesting" when I needed something, which meant I'd use affirmations, visualization, vision boards, vision casting, and other New Age tools to willfully insist that God deliver what I wanted. Instead of trying to control, I started dropping to my knees in prayer. Reading through the book of Psalms, especially David's psalms, taught me to pour my heart out to God. I told Him *everything* and asked Him for help with everything.

Although we'd moved to a different home, the spiritual warfare had followed me. In desperation, I contacted a deliverance minister for help. After our expensive session by Skype, the spiritual warfare continued to haunt me, and I still depended on melatonin to sleep. Finally (when it should have been my first impulse), I turned to see what the Bible said about spiritual warfare, and I discovered three important weapons for spiritual warfare.

1. The Armor of God

The apostle Paul described the spiritual warfare that affects believers, and then described the Christian armor that equips us to stand up to these spiritual assaults in Ephesians 6:10–13. As the theologian Iaian M. Duguid wrote, "The armor of God is quite literally God's armor . . . . The armor God gives us to defend and protect against Satan's onslaught is the armor that he has already worn in the decisive battle on our behalf. We fight and stand firm against Satan only in the strength that comes from the victory that Christ has already won for us."

These are the components of the armor of God:

- **The Belt of Truth.** In practical terms, this means reading the Bible daily. The Bible is God's truth that equips us in all situations. We can see a reference to this belt in Isaiah 11:5.
- **The Breastplate of Righteousness.** This phrase is from Isaiah 59:17, and it means to have faith in the righteousness that was imputed to you by Jesus' work on the cross. Professor Duguid wrote, "When you see that the righteousness obtained for us on the cross gives us profound security in God's love and powerful motivation against sin, you can see why Paul describes righteousness as our breastplate in our fight against the devil."

- **Shoes of the Gospel of Peace.** This comes from the passage about the beautiful feet of the one who delivers good news (the gospel means "good news") from Isaiah 52:7. This refers to obeying the Great Commission (Matthew 28:19–20) and getting out there and spreading the good news of the gospel far and wide. Spiritual warfare is often Satan's attempt to silence Christians so they won't spread the gospel.

- **The Shield of Faith.** "Faith protects us from Satan's attacks because of what faith enables to take hold of, namely, the power and protection of God Himself. Faith points our eyes toward the *promises of God*. When the evil one throws his flaming darts at you that say, 'God doesn't really care about you, or this bad thing wouldn't be happening,' faith puts out the fire," explained Professor Duguid.

- **The Helmet of Salvation.** This means having confident assurance that you are saved by the free gift that comes to us by faith in Christ. We can see this helmet in Isaiah 59:17. Duguid wrote that this kind of solid hope is a practical kind of helmet, as opposed to wrestling with doubts about your eternal salvation, which leads to despair. Your solid hope in salvation protects you in the deepest, darkest valleys of your life by reminding you of God's power and His care for you.

- **The Sword of the Spirit.** The final part of the armor is the Bible, which is the sword of the Spirit, just as Jesus used Scripture to defeat the devil in the wilderness (Matthew 4:1–11). Memorizing Bible verses (both the words and their meaning) gives you ammunition against the schemes of the devil.[3]

2. The Spoken Word of God

Just as Jesus' spoken word was powerful in defeating the devil . . . God's Word is also powerful when heard or read aloud. Michael and I listen to a Bible book each evening as we're falling asleep. Our favorite book to listen to is the gospel of John. If I was experiencing severe spiritual warfare, I'd play audios of the Bible throughout the day.

3. The Garment of Praise

I'd wake up feeling a heaviness upon me, and I couldn't shake it during the day. So, I turned to the Bible for help and found an answer in the King James Version of Isaiah 61:3, which discusses exchanging the garment of praise for the spirit of heaviness. When I first read that, I exclaimed, "The spirit of heaviness—*that* describes what I'm feeling!" Then, I set about researching what the "garment of praise" incorporated, and I found several commentators who said it involved sincerely praising God. I wrote out everything for which I was grateful to God, and I started silently saying that list of praise to God each morning. The heaviness lifted and hasn't returned!

These methods helped to considerably reduce the spiritual warfare I was experiencing, but there was more for me to learn. If you've ever read C. S. Lewis's classic book *The Screwtape Letters*,[4] then you know how demons can try to influence your thoughts. Well, I was on the receiving end of this type of warfare.

What I learned is that the devil tries to tempt you into sinning by reassuring you that God doesn't really care if you sin and you'll feel better if you sin. Besides, he'll emphasize: you deserve it! Then, when you give in to this temptation, *Bam!* The devil hits you with guilt and starts chiding you and telling you that God will never love or forgive you. "No one will listen to you, and no one will love you," says the devil.

There's a sorrow that comes from believing these lies from the devil, and succumbing to his temptations is followed by heavy guilt. This is called "worldly sorrow," and it's based on the devil's evil lies so that you won't feel worthy of fulfilling the Great Commission, which is Jesus' commandment for Christians to share the gospel worldwide: "Go therefore and make disciples of all nations, baptizing them in the name of the Father and of the Son and of the Holy Spirit, teaching them to observe all that I have commanded you." (Matthew 28:19–20).

The contrast to worldly sorrow is called "godly sorrow," which is a righteous form of sorrow when the Holy Spirit convicts you of sinful behavior. The Holy Spirit will never put you down with a guilt trip, like the devil does, but the Holy Spirit will pressure you to get back on track and leave sinful actions behind.

The devil tried to convince me that I was worthless because of my sinful past and that God could never use me for His glory. I almost fell for this lie, until I realized that the Bible is filled with stories of God using sinful people! Reading the ancestral lineage of Jesus is like reading a who's who of sinners. For example, God used Jacob's granddaughter-in-law Tamar, who pretended to be a prostitute and tricked Judah into sleeping with her. Their union resulted in twin sons, one of whom was Perez, who's an ancestor of Jesus (Genesis 38:6–29; Matthew 1:3; Luke 3:33).

Then, there's the Samaritan woman at the well, married five times and finally living with a man out of wedlock. Her ill repute meant that she went to the well alone, without the other women of the town. After she met Jesus, the Samaritan woman was one of the first Gentile evangelists to spread the word about Jesus (John 4:1–45).

Rahab is another example of God using sinful people for His plan of redemption. Rahab is described with the Hebrew word for *harlot*, which many commentators believe means she was either a prostitute or the madam of a house of prostitution in the city of Jericho. Rahab was instrumental in helping the Israelites send spies into Canaan, to plan their strategies, and Rahab even lied to protect the Israelite spies from being discovered. Rahab is an unlikely choice for Jesus' ancestry, yet her story shows that God can and will use anyone He pleases for His glory. Rahab's son was Boaz, who married Ruth (Joshua 2:1–3; 6:17–25; Matthew 1:5; Hebrews 11:31; James 2:25).

Charles Spurgeon said that people who've come out of grievously sinful pasts make some of the best evangelists: "Give me great sinners to make great saints; they are glorious raw material for grace to work upon; and when you do get them saved, they will shake the very gates of hell. The ringleaders in Satan's camp make noble sergeants in the camp of Christ. These bravest of the brave are they."[5]

When I realized this, I prayed for the Holy Spirit's guidance to be revealed so that I could stop doing anything that was offending God (Psalm 139:23–24). The Holy Spirit convicted me to take a strong stand on social media against my previous work. People had only superficially heard me denounce the New Age, and I needed to be ultra-clear so there was no doubt. I needed to stop comforting people in their sins, and letting them believe that it was okay to practice divination, fortune-telling, mediumship, or witchcraft. Because it's not okay; it's sinful.

When I began posting bold messages on social media, the spiritual warfare reduced considerably. I posted clearly that my old angel cards can attract demons, and of course many people took offense and argued with me. But I also noticed that I was finally able to sleep without melatonin.

Spiritual warfare isn't always about the devil's retribution. Our sovereign God may allow a season of spiritual warfare to test us as He did with Job. God may also use spiritual warfare to humble and bend us to His will.

My posts and videos against the New Age were bold, and I asked people to not buy my old products and to burn or throw away my old products if they had them. Many people didn't understand that these denouncements were coming from a place of love, just as if I were warning someone that a speeding truck was heading their way.

My old friends, and some New Age family members, saw my evangelizing work as being "unloving." One family member informed me that Jesus would never talk this way and that if I was a real Christian, I would never put down other religions. That person had never read how Jesus spoke to the Pharisees. My relative gave me an ultimatum: either I stop evangelizing against the New Age or I wouldn't hear from him again. Since my relative and I had been extremely close when we were both in the New Age, it grieved my heart. However, I couldn't stay silent about the fact that my old products were spiritually toxic.

I felt like an ex–tobacco industry worker turned whistleblower who realized these products caused cancer. I made videos and wrote blogs, begging people not to buy New Age products anymore—including my own. With each blog and video, I discussed how the devil runs the New Age as his attempt to lure people away from God. Satan wants to fill hell with his victims, and he'll promise people anything—a soul mate, a new job, wealth, health, anything you want—to trick them into following him.

I warn people because I care and because I wish someone would've warned me back then. How would you feel to learn that you'd wasted fifty-eight years of your life? How would you feel to learn that you'd raised your children in a false religion? How would you feel to know that your books and teachings misled people? So, I warn everyone in the same way I wish someone had warned me back then.

Some people misunderstand my intentions for issuing these warnings against the New Age and false teachers. I've been accused of "hating on people," "being judgmental," "dividing the body," "being legalistic," and "not being a true Christian." Repeatedly, people have told me that Jesus would never have spoken out against the New Age or false teachers. I point them to Scripture, particularly Matthew 23, where Jesus pronounces woes upon the Pharisees, scribes, and other hypocritical false teachers of His day.

In the New Age, before reading the Gospels, I'd imagined Jesus to be a laid-back guy who continually said, "Peace be with you," and never challenged anyone. In my imagination, Jesus never judged anyone, but always smiled approvingly wherever He went. That's why I was so surprised to read Matthew 23:33, where Jesus called the hypocrites "serpents" and "a brood of vipers," going on to say, "How are you to escape being sentenced to hell?" Whoa! That doesn't sound very approving, does it?

If you hold a Jesus-loves-and-approves-of-everything-and-everyone viewpoint, I encourage you to read Matthew 23 for yourself. In the New Age, I held a very common belief called universalism, which means you think that everyone is going to heaven, as well as pluralism, which means that all paths lead to God. In universalism and pluralism, as long as you're a good person, you're golden. That's what I believed and taught, and it's probably what a large portion of the population believes.

I also believed and taught that hell was a myth, or perhaps a metaphor of having a hellishly awful life here on earth. One of my New Age friends said that the concept of a fiery hell was a scare tactic based on the fiery trash dumps in Gehenna, near Jerusalem during biblical times, almost like our parents today warning us that we'd be restricted to our room if we didn't behave. According to the New Age, people in biblical times would be warned that they'd be thrown in the fiery garbage dump. Well, I wish that hell was a myth, but according to the Bible, and especially according to Jesus, hell is more than real.

Do you see how perfectly the devil insulates deceived New Agers so they can't hear the gospel truth? New Agers don't believe in a literal devil, nor in hell. In fact, the fear of hell (or the distastefulness of the topic) is one of the reasons why people leave Christianity to go into the New Age. At my workshops, I talked to many former Catholics and ex-Christians who said they felt frightened or guilty when they'd attended church in the past. So, they started reading New Age books and attending New Age workshops because they preferred to hear teachers who claimed hell doesn't exist. There's something about hearing groups of people claim there's no hell that seems to validate that claim. Most popular New Age teachers ooze an authoritative and relatable persona that lulls you into feeling safe in your sinful lifestyle, believing there are no consequences.

Just as Satan cast doubt into Eve's mind—"Did God really say that? Oh, God didn't really mean that!"—so, too, does the devil try to get New Agers to doubt that God sends anyone to hell. The devil portrays God and Jesus as all-accepting, always understanding, and always inclusive. I understand, because that's what I used to believe too.

I'm sure I'll get letters about this section of the book from people who are certain that God is all love and no wrath. And I will reply to those letters that I completely understand why they believe that, because that's the party line for the New Age that I used to believe. The focus is on "God is love" and ignoring that God is also holy. And our holy God cannot be in the presence of sin. He is 100 percent pure, and sin is 100 percent evil. God is light, and in Him is no darkness at all (1 John 1:5).

When we sin (which means to break any of God's Ten Commandments, such as lying, stealing, having lustful or covetous thoughts), we shatter our relationship with God. Jesus came to earth as a mediator between sinful humanity and God. God the Father, Jesus the Son, and the Holy Spirit are all three persons of our one triune God.

When Jesus said, "I am the way, and the truth, and the life. No one comes to the Father except through me" (John 14:6), Jesus meant that He is the *only* gateway for sinful people like you and me to be in the presence of God. There are no other ways to reach heaven, unless you're 100 percent sinless—which no one is, unless you're Jesus.

As I mentioned earlier, and it bears repeating: I find the following passage to be one of the most frightening sections of the Bible. In this passage, Jesus has just finished explaining that a tree that doesn't bear fruit will be cut down and thrown into the fire (Matthew 7:19). Then Jesus says:

> "Not everyone who says to me, 'Lord, Lord,' will enter the kingdom of heaven, but the one who does the will of my Father who is in heaven. On that day many will say to me, 'Lord, Lord, did we not prophesy in your name, and cast out demons in your name, and do many mighty works in your name?' And then will I declare to them, 'I never knew you; depart from me, you workers of lawlessness.'"
> (Matthew 7:21–23)

Can you imagine standing before Jesus after you've died, and He casts you away because He doesn't know who you are? How absolutely terrifying! This is one of many reasons why we must develop a close personal relationship with Jesus. We must cling to Him like a koala bear clings to a eucalyptus tree. We must commit every minute of every day to following Jesus as our Lord and Savior.

Did you know that Jesus talked about hell more than He discussed the topic of heaven? That's because He loves us enough to tell us the truth and warn us. When my kids were young, we lived near a busy street, and I had to warn them several times to stay out of the street. I didn't warn them about traffic because I was judging my kids. I wasn't giving these warnings because I was legalistic. My warnings about traffic were because I love my kids and want them to be safe.

As Charles Spurgeon said, "In hell, there is no hope. They have not even the hope of dying—the hope of being annihilated. They are forever—forever—lost!"[6]

If you're currently in the New Age, I know that the New Age seems to offer qualities that Christianity does not. But at what cost? I pray that if you are following New Age practices, you will repent and turn to Jesus now while there's still time.

What I also haven't mentioned yet is that back in 2016, before my big Jesus experience, Michael began watching YouTube videos from people who claimed to have had near-death experiences (NDE) visits to hell. In the New Age (both Michael and I were in the New Age back then), it's common to obsessively watch NDE videos about visits to heaven. In these NDEs, the person says they're met by their relatives and shown around a gorgeous garden filled with light, joy, and love. These videos seem to confirm that everyone goes to heaven and no one is excluded.

However, very few people watch the large number of videos from people who claim they had an NDE visit to hell. I certainly hadn't, until Michael started to watch them. Out of curiosity, and remember this is before I'd studied the Gospels carefully, I began viewing testimonies from people who said they'd gone to hell after a drug overdose, suicide attempt, and other dark circumstances.

Hell is a place of torment because it's a place of God's wrath that we all deserve, if Jesus had not taken the punishment for us. There's no rest from the endless torture from which you can never escape. Each person described unbearable heat with unquenchable thirst, hearing thousands of people screaming for help, and the stench of burning sulfur. Every moment you're tortured by demons, chewing on you as if you're a meal. You pray for relief, but there is none. You repent, but it's too late.

Some people believe these NDEs are imaginary products of a dying brain, and they could be. Jesus said that no one has ever ascended into heaven, except He who descended from heaven (John 3:13). And the author of Hebrews said that it's appointed for us to die once, and after that comes judgment (Hebrews 9:27).

These verses are powerful arguments against reincarnation, by the way. I used to believe in reincarnation, and even had some mind-blowing past life regression sessions with "memories" that I corroborated historically. I now realize that the devil creates these false memories by planting visions in your mind. After all, the belief in reincarnation keeps New Agers from repenting, because you believe you get unlimited future chances to make your life right with God. You don't. It's part of the devil's evil scheme to get you into his lair in hell, by preventing you from salvation.

When Jesus said, "It is finished" on the cross (John 19:30), He meant that God's plan of redemption had been fulfilled through Him. There won't be future crucifixions of Jesus. If reincarnation *were* true (which it's *not*), then the painful suffering of Jesus on the cross wouldn't have been necessary.

FOURTEEN

Making New Friends

My former New Age publisher has an online radio station, and I was a host of a weekly show on their station for about fifteen years. One day on the show, I mentioned that I'd thrown away my deity statues. This was a big change for me, as my home had previously been filled with statues of Quan Yin (the Buddhist "goddess of compassion"). I must have had twenty statues of her, which I repented for when I disposed of the images. People who heard me discuss this on the radio expressed confusion: "But don't all spiritual paths lead to heaven?" and "But aren't we all worshiping the same God in different ways?" That's the way I used to think too.

The more I spoke openly about changes that stemmed from my conversion to Christianity, the more confused and upset people who followed my work seemed to become. Some people even angrily confronted my sons and daughters-in-law about my conversion.

My New Age friends stopped calling and emailing, and I didn't hear from many people on my birthday. During my New Age touring years, I traveled with friends, many of whom I helped get publishing contracts. We were very close, until I started speaking out against the New Age. I'm not the type to chase after people and beg them to come back. So, my social and support circle shrank to my immediate family and my childhood friends. I was lonely and tired of dealing with spiritual warfare and the cruel backlash videos and blogs being posted about me.

I took some comfort in the fact that Jesus promised this would happen. Jesus said, "Blessed are you when people hate you and when they exclude you and revile you and spurn your name as evil, on account of the Son of Man!" *The Son of Man* was a name for Jesus, who reassured us that persecution would happen (Luke 6:22). Jesus also said, "If the world hates you, know that it has hated me before it hated you" (John 15:18).

Still, I was lonely. I wanted friends who understood my love for Jesus and who wouldn't judge me for my New Age past.

One day I saw a video on YouTube from an ex–New Ager named Steven Bancarz, who once was a famous blogger on a popular spirit-science (metaphysics and consciousness studies) website. Steven was raised in a Christian home, but he had drifted away because of his interest in UFOs and Eastern meditation. He became wealthy, popular, and successful as a spirit-science blogger, but his mother continued to pray for Steven's salvation. Her prayers were answered one evening when Steven had a strong sense of the presence of Jesus. Just as with my January 7, 2017, experience, Steven was transformed by Jesus' presence. He didn't see a vision, but he was left *knowing* for certain that the Bible is true.

Steven shut down his popular website, sold his home, moved back home to his parents' basement, and committed to following Jesus as his Lord and Savior. I reached out to Steven and we became friends, which we are to this day. Since his conversion happened a year before mine, he was able to counsel me about how to share my testimony publicly. Steven's YouTube videos detailing his transformation gave me the courage to make videos of my own journey leaving the New Age.

I will always appreciate Steven being there for me in my early years, especially since some New Agers told him to not friend me, as they doubted my motivations for being a Christian. He also sweetly gifted me with an *ESV Study Bible* to edify Scripture reading. Even though we don't always agree about theology, Steven and I do agree that the New Age is a doctrine of demons and that Jesus is our Lord and Savior.

Steven has been very supportive of my walk with Christ, including us making some videos together of our testimonies and practical considerations for those who are leaving the New Age. I also contributed an article to his helpful book on the topic, *The Second Coming of the New Age.*[1]

While on Facebook one day, I typed "New Age to Christianity" into the search bar. I was amazed that a private Facebook group popped up! I joined the group and was greeted by the administrator, Melissa Dougherty. She'd started the group when her sister got involved with the New Age movement. Melissa had been raised with Christian Science influences, and she'd gotten involved with Word of Faith and prosperity teachings. Melissa always thought of herself as a Christian, and was surprised to learn that some of the teachers she'd followed were New Age and not Christian. *But they used Bible verses!* Both Melissa and I learned the hard way that false prophets often quote the Bible with twisted Scripture. After all, the devil quoted Scripture while trying to tempt Jesus (Matthew 4:1–11).

I was so happy to meet Melissa and join her ex–New Ager support group! I was eager to meet others who'd come out of deception and discuss how to overcome some of the issues unique to that type of conversion. However, there were only fifty people in her group at that time, and people would only post once or twice a week. Melissa later told me that she was praying about shutting down the group because it was so slow, right before I joined.

Desiring more fellowship with ex–New Agers, I decided to open my own Facebook group with a woman I'd recently met on another Christian site. I announced the new group on my radio show and social media pages, and we quickly swelled to three thousand members. I got what I'd asked for: an active group! The trouble was that the woman who was coadministering the group with me turned out to have a completely different approach to Christianity than I did.

While I was posting about the necessity for Bible study, she'd post that the Bible was filled with errors and that it wasn't necessary to study. I'd post suggestions for finding a church, while she'd post that church attendance wasn't necessary. She also angrily confronted me and said that I was wrong if I wasn't a universalist. As you'll recall, a universalist is someone who believes that everyone goes to heaven, no matter what their faith or lifestyle. Once again, I'd fallen into the deception of believing that the term *Christian* meant that everyone believed similarly. I prayed to not do that anymore.

One day in Melissa's group, our friend Taz Bright posted a powerful blog about the importance of church attendance. Taz detailed all the suffering the apostles and the early church had gone through, which afforded us the ability today to attend church. I was so inspired by his blog post that I shared it with my newly formed group.

Well, the reaction that blog received in my group would have led you to believe that I'd posted something with cussing and raging hatred. Right away, the group divided into the churched and unchurched, with me and the other administrator in the crosshairs. Group members furiously posted about why we should or shouldn't attend church. It got very heated and nasty in no time!

If the administrators had been aligned, we could've handled the situation. But with two administrators believing in opposite ways, a big division happened instead. We decided to close the group and go our separate ways. I asked people who wanted to join me to meet me at Melissa's New Age to Christianity group, which swelled by fifteen hundred people that day.

Melissa and I developed a close friendship, and she was very supportive during those early days of my conversion. I was still wobbly, like a newborn colt, unsure of my footing as I filmed videos or wrote blogs. Melissa would sweetly text me daily encouragements and check to see how I was doing. She became my sister in Christ, and we grew and learned together. In the early days, we also met in online prayer groups with the administrators from Steven Bancarz's "Reasons for Jesus" Facebook page, including Stephan, David, John, Jovan, Brie, and others.

In addition, I'd joined groups on Facebook about detecting deception in the Christian church, as I was dismayed to find so many New Age practices in churches. The NAR (New Apostolic Reformation) heresy group on Facebook helped me learn what and whom to avoid. For example, one NAR church teaches that the New Age "stole" their practices from Christianity, so they are reinstating these practices (such as having a spirit guide, going into trances, auras, power objects, clairvoyance, clairaudience, "Christian tarot cards," and Eastern forms of meditation) in their church.[2]

I was shocked to find the same practices I'd just left behind in the New Age were in churches that claimed to be Christian! Watching the events on some of the church stages was virtually identical to the mind-body-spirit seminars I'd participated in for twenty-five years. The only apparent difference was that we paid income taxes in the New Age.

I also learned that some Christian music originated from churches that taught similarly to the Christian Science and New Age heresies I'd just left. While the old-time hymn writers weren't always without issues themselves, the concern with some modern Christian music was how it enticed people into unbiblical churches that taught heresies such as kenosis (that Jesus emptied His godly divinity when He came to earth, and that He was just a mortal man during His earthly ministry).

Melissa and I began interviewing "discernment ministry" leaders (people who teach how to avoid spiritual deception) on my YouTube channel, so that we could learn more about how to avoid deception. Our first interview was with Ray Comfort, whose video *Hell's Best-Kept Secret* had helped me when my brother Ken recommended it to me. Ray's book *Banana Man* had also encouraged me to keep evangelizing publicly despite the public backlash. *Banana Man* is Ray's autobiographical account of witnessing to famous atheists, and how he withstands the hatred he receives. I kept thinking, *If Ray can handle the hatred, then so can I.* And, of course, Jesus promised this reaction when He said, "If the world hates you, know that it has hated me before it hated you" (John 15:18).

My other prayer with our YouTube videos was to introduce our audience members to Christian authors. When I was in the New Age, I was always struck by the small number of authors we followed. There were probably twelve to twenty New Age authors who wrote the majority of the books and gave the majority of New Age workshops. We all basically said the same thing from different angles.

Many of the people on social media and YouTube who run discernment ministries have come out of deception themselves. It's such a horrible feeling to realize you've been deceived and that you could have ended up in hell because you weren't saved by having faith in the true Jesus and the real gospel. Discernment ministers, including Chris Rosebrough, Justin Peters, Costi Hinn, Warren B. Smith, Marcia Montenegro, and Amy Spreeman, teach from their own real-world experiences with previously being deceived themselves.

Kicked Out

We moved from Hawaii to the Pacific Northwest (PNW) in November 2017. The shock of going from the year-round warmth of Hawaii to the dark, rainy winter of the Pacific Northwest felt like being exiled to

Siberia or something. I love the region now, but that first winter was brutal! I missed my friends and my animals in Hawaii. I missed having the opportunity to swim in the warm ocean waters.

The intense hatred from New Agers and the spiritual warfare coming at me, combined with the frigid PNW temperatures, led me to become depressed. I started overeating and gained so much weight so quickly that people asked if my thyroid was okay. (I'd had it recently checked, so I knew it was overeating, not metabolism, making me swell.)

Soon after we moved, I made a social media post with the verses from Deuteronomy 18:10–12. In the comment of the post, I said that this was the Bible passage that had led me to quit the New Age practices.

About an hour later, I received an email from the president of my publishing house informing me that I'd crossed the line with this post. He was concerned that I'd offend witches with these Bible verses that condemned divination, fortune-telling, omen interpretation, mediumship, and witchcraft. Since the publisher had newly begun printing witchcraft books, they didn't want to upset their customers.

He told me I was fired.

I'd been working with that publisher for twenty-five years and was their top-selling author. We'd traveled around the world together, and here I was getting fired by email three weeks before Christmas. I was losing my radio show, my website, and my publishing contracts.

When I'd first started with the publisher, they only printed books about health, inspiration, and positive affirmations. They wouldn't even use the word *psychic* or other New Age terms in their books. Here they were, twenty-five years later, printing witchcraft books! This showed me the progressive nature of deception. When I first opened a New Age book in the 1990s, I stopped reading when I realized the author, Shakti Gawain, hadn't mentioned Jesus in her book. Years later, as my deception progressed, the name of Jesus was no longer a criterion determining whether or not I'd read a book.

The progression of deception is dangerous. R. C. Sproul wrote, "Sinfulness does not stand still, but grows worse," in view of Romans 6:19, which says that lawlessness leads to more lawlessness.[3] Several Christian women have sent me their testimonies of how they'd initially entered the New Age with my sweet-and-innocent-seeming angel cards. Once they were in the New Age, they kept going and eventually got involved in darker practices, such as Wicca and witchcraft. Only by the grace of God did they escape New Age deception and turn to Jesus.

The devil entices people into deception with promises of physical healings, finding your soul mate, experiencing peace, or manifesting wealth. Once you're hooked in by his temptations, the devil continues to lead you deeper into his pit of deception.

I felt horrible that I'd been used by the devil as a gateway into the New Age, and I was only comforted by seeing how God was using my testimony to encourage backslidden Christians to return to Jesus. Lots of ex–New Agers write me now, saying that my testimony was the final straw that got them back to church and out of the New Age. All glory to God for using my testimony for His kingdom!

Even though I was hurt by the way my publisher fired me, it was ultimately for the best. A long-term business relationship is like a marriage, and the Bible tells Christians not to be yoked together with unbelievers. "For what partnership has righteousness with lawlessness? Or what fellowship has light with darkness?" Paul wrote in 2 Corinthians 6:14. This verse would strengthen me against temptation later when I received several lucrative business propositions from other New Age companies. I turned down their offers and trusted God to meet my needs. Which He has—thank you, Lord!

Right after my conversion, I had written a couple of books and even new cards that I believed at that time were Christian. They certainly were in the right direction, but as a baby Christian, my theological understanding wasn't solid enough yet for me to write biblically correct books. Those publications didn't sell very well, which also added to my publisher's distaste with my conversion. My overall sales and popularity continued to plummet, and they were done with me.

When I was in the New Age, I was obsessed with gaining more followers for me and my books. Now, since conversion, my whole focus is on Jesus' followers. All glory to God!

The One-Year Bible Support Group

A month after being fired, I recalled a long-forgotten memory from childhood when a friend in my neighborhood invited me to attend Vacation Bible School (VBS) at his family's Baptist church. We were only about six or seven years old. I remembered that we'd all sat in chairs in a big circle, holding illustrated children's Bibles on our laps. We'd listen to the Bible stories being read by the adults. I remembered being enthralled and not wanting to give the Bible back when each VBS day ended. Interestingly, my mother also suddenly remembered my going to that childhood VBS class.

That VBS was all about the Bible. There weren't any skits, loud music, or other entertainment. And I'd loved it! What a contrast to modern VBS at many churches today. While in Hawaii, I'd helped to decorate and serve as a Bible teacher for the Episcopal church VBS. At our new church in the Pacific Northwest, I was asked to be the VBS director, as their former director had moved away and they were in a pinch to find someone new. Michael and I worked on making cardboard palm trees and sailboat decorations together, to make the sanctuary look like a shipwrecked island to match the VBS "Shipwrecked" theme.

Recalling the simple, Bible-focused VBS of my childhood made me wonder what would have happened if I'd continued to go to that Baptist church. What would my life—and my children's lives—have been like if I'd been saved at an early age and raised as a Christian?

I had deep regrets about the bad choices I'd made in my life, anger toward my mother for raising my brother and me in the apostate Christian Science church, and was upset that no one had clearly explained the gospel to me earlier. To be fair, my brother Ken and his wife, Jann, said that they'd tried to share the gospel with me many times in the past, but I had always shut them down.

In the New Age, Michael and I had spent money faster than we made it, we owed back taxes, and I was too old to reenter the job market. My previous New Age business had employed several people, including my son and daughter-in-law, who depended upon this income. Michael started a new business to bring in some income. I prayed for God's help with provision, although a part of me felt undeserving of His favor because of the sinful nature of my life before salvation. During that time, several people I'd known in the New Age offered me business opportunities that I had to decline because I was done with the New Age. I was leaning on God.

I'd recently finished reading *The One-Year Bible* that my son Grant had sent to me, and I was already beginning to read it through for the second time. I kept getting a thought to share daily Bible reading with others. After all, I'd really enjoyed sharing the Bible with the kids during VBS.

I wasn't qualified to teach about the Bible then, but I could share commentaries of each day's Bible reading. I inquired on social media if other people would be interested in joining in such a group. I explained that we'd meet at a specific time daily during a live video posted on my Instagram account. When several people said they'd love to join me, I encouraged them to purchase their own copy of *The One Year Bible*.

The group was free of charge without any financial compensation, so I was really leaning on God, knowing that I'd be involved in researching and teaching daily without pay for one whole year.

We began the group's first meeting on December 30, 2017. Since people were joining from the Southern Hemisphere (Australia, New

Zealand, etc.), where it was one day ahead of my time zone, we'd always work one day ahead. We'd discuss the January 1 Bible reading on December 31, which was January 1 in the Southern Hemisphere.

During the first live video meeting, I explained that we'd be meeting for 365 days in a row throughout 2018. We'd all read that day's Bible passages on our own; then we'd gather online as I read commentaries on those sections for each day. It was a big undertaking! My friends Melissa and Stephan sweetly agreed to be backup group leaders for any days that I couldn't make it, but it turned out that I was able to film each day of 2018 after all.

A lovely woman named Nicole Neville volunteered to administrate a private Facebook group for those attending the daily videos, and so the "One Year Bible Support Group" was born!

Each afternoon, I'd collect and read commentaries for that evening's video broadcast. My husband was incredibly understanding that my afternoons and evenings were filled for an entire year, and that I wasn't being paid to do this project.

Right away there was an issue, though, because people had purchased two different versions of *The One Year Bible*. In the "chronological" version, people read the Bible in the order that the books were written. That version stays in the Old Testament through its completion and then starts on the New Testament after several months. The other version (the one I'd read) gives you an Old Testament passage, New Testament passage, psalm, and proverb to read each day.

How would we handle the daily readings and commentaries for the group when some people had the chronological version? After praying and spending a few days facilitating the group, we hit our stride. I'd read commentaries for the chronological version in half of each night's video, then read commentaries for the other version in the other half of each night's video.

This required me to be prepared each evening with commentaries for two different versions of *The One Year Bible*. This double duty pushed me in a good way, though. It forced me to dig deep into the Bible so I could explain difficult passages and time lines to others.

First, I had to figure out which commentaries were reliable. There are so many out there, and some of them conflict. After trying a few different commentaries for a couple of months, we soon found that Pastor David Guzik's commentaries and the GotQuestions.org website provided answers for most of the questions we had. I also used the *NKJV Cultural Backgrounds Study Bible* to help understand the historical-cultural context of the Bible passages we were studying.

Each night, we'd have approximately three thousand people worldwide joining in live and on rebroadcast. I took the responsibility very seriously, and I prayed before every broadcast to accurately convey God's Word. I didn't want to be deceived or deceive anyone ever again! Looking back, my first two or three months were not as theologically strong as the rest of the year. Fortunately, God is in charge, and the letters I receive show that people from that group continue to read and study the Bible to this day.

Facilitating the One Year Bible Support Group for 365 consecutive days (including holidays, my birthday, while I was traveling, and one time when I caught a cold) was challenging but very fruitful. It pushed me to understand concepts that had previously been fuzzy. It made me learn how to explain challenging sections of the Bible. The experience also helped me to grasp the biblical time line, especially the exile, which had seemed confusing to me the first time I'd read the Bible. (*Why do they keep talking about going to Babylon? Didn't they just go to Babylon in the previous book?*)

The experience also encouraged me to keep going with my Bible studies. I *love* learning about the Bible! I decided to enroll in seminary to study biblical theology. Many people have asked me why I'm going to seminary, and a few have worriedly asked whether I'm planning on pastoring a church or something. No, that's not my calling (1 Timothy 2:12). My motivation is purely the love of studying the Bible; to help me avoid eisegesis, twisting Scripture, or being deceived again; and to encourage others to read the Bible. I would love to write Bible study books and blogs about studying the Bible.

Michael and I trusted that if seminary was God's will, then the time and cost of seminary would be provided. I also prayed that if it was God's will, I'd be accepted into a particular seminary I liked because it emphasized the inerrancy of the Bible (some seminaries teach doubts about the Bible's inerrancy and often ruin students' faith). I also liked that the seminary was gospel centered and geographically near my home so I could attend classes in person.

The application process was daunting, with requirements for all my school transcripts plus letters of recommendation from pastors and friends in ministry. Since Michael and I had only recently moved to the area, I was concerned about asking my new pastor for a recommendation. Thank the Lord, my pastor agreed, and my new Christian friends also provided recommendations.

In January 2019, I began full-time studies in a combination of online and in-person classes. Each semester I pay for my classes with a credit card, and then Michael and I trust that the cost of seminary will be provided. So far, it has been!

Sitting in those classrooms as a sixty-year-old woman was initially intimidating, surrounded by twenty-five-year-old future pastors. I've found that Christians with a pastor's heart are warm and friendly, however, so my seminary social experiences have been positive.

Plus, as I mature and grow as a Christian, I'm easier to get along with. Initially I was suffering from some post-traumatic stress disorder symptoms. Realizing that my whole belief system had been built on the devil's lies was traumatic, and transitioning from New Age into Christianity was confusing at first. I didn't know who I was, why I was here, or what I was supposed to do. When I was first saved, my vocabulary still sounded like a New Ager's, which confused my new Christian friends (except the ex–New Agers, who understood why I still used New Age terms).

I was also easily triggered by deception and would react with righteous anger if someone would discuss doing a New Age practice at a Christian church. I'd then try to teach that person about the deception, with too much intensity. I was like an ex-smoker going around telling people not to smoke, which is good advice except that some people just want to enjoy inhaling smoke instead of listening to a lecture. The truth is that I unfortunately pushed some people away with my extreme attempts to warn them about encroaching New Age deception. They'd shut down or avoid me, so my warnings would fall on deaf ears. I'm learning how to dial it back a bit, to recognize when I'm triggered, and to be a better communicator in my discernment work.

Spending time daily studying the Bible has definitely helped me, as has attending a solid church and being a part of the fellowship community. Michael and I looked for a church that was centered on the gospel; that only played music from classic hymns (since many modern Christian songs are licensed from apostate churches);[4] where the pastor met the qualifications of 1 Timothy 3:1–7; that offered opportunities for Bible study and volunteer work; that was worship-filled; and that did not offer New Age components, such as yoga classes (including "Christian yoga"),[5] the Enneagram personality test,[6] or prophets who were more like psychic readers.

Once we held these criteria prayerfully in mind, we found several churches from which to choose. Unlike the stereotypes I'd previously held about born-again Christians, the Christians in our congregation are filled with the Holy Spirit. There's nothing dry, dusty, or boring about church. In fact, it's exactly what I'd been seeking.

Afterword

Since reading and rereading the entire Bible, I no longer have that gnawing sense of searching for the secret. I was convinced that the answers were in some old antiquarian book somewhere. And they were! The answers were clearly spelled out in the Bible.

Each Bible story contains nuggets of spiritual wisdom that we can apply to our lives, including learning who God is, what He wants (and doesn't want) from us, and how Jesus on the cross gave us direct access to our heavenly Father and assurance of eternal life.

I love the Holy Spirit's convictions nowadays, but as a baby Christian I was confused. It took a while to recognize the difference between the Holy Spirit humbling me and the enemy's attempts at humiliation. The Holy Spirit is like a loving parent warning a child to stop running with scissors. The enemy, in contrast, schemes to destroy your relationship with God by convincing you that you're unlovable and unforgivable.

The Bible fillets us like a surgeon's scalpel, exposing our dark secrets to the sunlight of God's love. Hebrews 4:12–13 says, "For the word of God is living and active, sharper than any two-edged sword, piercing to the division of soul and spirit, of joints and of marrow, and discerning the thoughts and intentions of the heart. And no creature is hidden from his sight, but all are naked and exposed to the eyes of him to whom we must give account."

For those with control issues, being exposed by the Bible sounds frightening and uncomfortable! Yet, think of someone who's been suffering with an unknown diagnosis. Finally, that person finds a doctor who can identify and treat his or her condition. Wouldn't that person gladly give the doctor permission to conduct invasive tests? Wouldn't it be a huge relief to get answers? Well, it's the same with allowing the Holy Spirit to reveal your deepest fears, secrets, and flaws as you read Scripture. *You can trust God's Spirit to take good care of you!*

I've bared my soul in this book so that those in deception may recognize some of the processes I went through before and after salvation. I'm not going to sugarcoat it: being a Christian isn't easy. However, it's the *only* way to find answers, assurance, and lasting peace.

As I write this, I'm preparing for my next semester in seminary. Michael and I are trusting that God will continue to provide enough to pay for my books and classes, in addition to keeping a roof over our heads. Michael started a new business, and God blesses him with enough work to pay our bills and enough time off to allow him to do volunteer work. Thomas Nelson, the publisher of the book you're now holding, offered me a book contract that not only helped to cover seminary tuition costs but answered my prayer about using my past to glorify God. Thank you, Lord!

Our life today is humble and centers around volunteering. Before salvation, I did volunteer work but immediately broadcast it on social media to get "likes." Since salvation, Michael and I do volunteer work because we're called to help. We both wish we could volunteer full-time and not have to work for an income.

We no longer post about our volunteer work on social media, or even talk about it much with our friends and family. Jesus said:

> "When you give to the needy, sound no trumpet before you, as the hypocrites do in the synagogues and in the streets, that they may be praised by others. Truly, I say to you, they have received their reward. But when you give to the needy, do not let your left hand know what your right hand is doing, so that your giving may be in secret. And your Father who sees in secret will reward you." (Matthew 6:2–4)

My family and friends who've stuck with me through my conversion remark that I seem much more patient and loving now. I certainly feel that way too. The Bible promises that our old heart of stone will be replaced by a new heart when we're saved (Ezekiel 11:19), and that's exactly what it feels like. I cry more easily, am more empathetic, and obeying God is my top priority. My days are spent reading and studying the Bible, and I pray that I can write more books about what I'm learning and applying.

One thing's for sure: I will continue to pray and compare everything to the Bible so that I'm deceived no more.

Appreciation and Apologies

Thank you to everyone who has supported and come alongside me through my conversion from New Age to Christianity. It has been challenging, to say the least, to have my life transformed at age fifty-eight after a lifetime of deception. Your friendship, prayers, and support have encouraged and lifted me up, and I appreciate you.

Of course, all glory goes to our triune God, who through mercy and grace plucked me out of deception and opened my eyes to the Bible. I'm eternally grateful for this free gift, which I didn't earn or deserve—thank you, Lord! Thank you also, Lord, for giving me the strength to write this confessional testimony book exposing the lies of the enemy and baring my soul. All glory to God!

Thank you to my husband, Michael, who transitioned with me out of the New Age, and who now prays, attends church, and volunteers alongside me. Many people mistakenly believe that you somehow coerced me into Christianity, when the truth is that you sweetly agreed to accompany me to church when Jesus was pursuing me out of the

New Age. Together, we left the New Age behind. Michael, I love you and our Jesus-centered marriage!

Thank you to my son Grant and his wife, Melissa, for enduring hateful letters that the public sent to you after my conversion and for sticking by my side no matter what. *That's love!* I'm so sorry that my conversion caused you stress, hardship, and persecution. And thank you, Grant, for sending me *The One Year Bible* NLT, which was the first Bible I read in its entirety. I love you both and my sweet grandchildren so much!

Thank you to my brother Ken and sister-in-law, Jann, both born-again Christians who I unfortunately avoided and misjudged during my apostate years, but who nonetheless prayed for me along with their Bible study participants. I love and appreciate you both so much, and I still grieve over the lost years when we could have been praying together.

To my son Charles: I love you very much!

Thank you to my parents. Although I wish we'd followed the Presbyterian denomination of Dad's side of the family, I trust that God is now using the Christian Science path that you chose, for His glory in exposing the darkness of false teachings and pointing people to His Word.

Thank you to Pastor Alistair Begg and the Christian Satellite Network, for broadcasting a sermon in January 2015 called "Itching Ears" (2 Timothy 4:3–4), which began the unraveling of my deception and planted seeds in me. I am weeping tears of gratitude as I write this now.

Thank you to Pastor Chris Rosebrough of "Fighting for the Faith," for showing me the importance of comparing all teachings against Scripture, and for leading me away from the false teachers I started to follow as a brand-new Christian. I appreciate your support and encouragement very much!

Thank you to Warren and Joy Smith, for your friendship, support, and your book *The Light That Was Dark,* which helped me to see that *A Course in Miracles,* which I'd been studying for twenty years, is a doctrine of demons and the opposite of the Bible. Because of your work, I threw away my copies of *A Course in Miracles* and began the process of throwing away everything that was unbiblical.

Thank you to Dr. Michael Heiser for your support and encouragement, and for writing the book *Angels,* which I wish I could've read many years ago.

Thank you to Tanner and Hillary Johnsrud, former Christian Science practitioners who are now born-again Christians, with a forthcoming book from Tanner. Thank you, Tanner, for helping me with research about the spiritualism and mediumship conducted by Mary Baker Eddy. Praise Jesus for saving us out of that heresy!

Thank you to Steven Kozar for pointing me toward a source of research for the connection between the Word-Faith movement and Christian Science. I appreciate your dedication to researching and exposing false teachings and pointing everyone to Scripture.

Thank you to my amazing mother-in-law, Dawn, for your prayers and support. Thank you to my stepdaughter, Ashley, for your continuous love and support. Thank you to my nieces and nephews-in-law for your prayers and support: Candice, Caitlin, Caryn, Chris, Sean, and Josh.

Thank you to my lifelong friends Anita, Silvia, and Melinda for sticking with me through all those years when I was steeped in darkness: *you are true friends whom I love so much!* I also appreciate the friends I met in the New Age who've stayed friends with me, even through the times when you received a hateful backlash for your association with me, including Sherry, Andrew, Becky, Angie, Elena (who is now a born-again Christian!), and Alessandra.

Thank you to Steven Bancarz, Melissa Dougherty, Stephan Johnson, Warren Smith, and Joy Smith for your support during the early moments of my conversion. I was like a newborn horse walking on wobbly legs as I first came out of the New Age, and you all tirelessly supported my early sanctification process. I also appreciate that you didn't allow the wave of hate coming against me to dissuade you from our friendship. Thank you to my new sisters and brothers in Christ, including Katie Beim-Esche, Danny Cooper, Lindsay Davis-Knotts and Zack Knotts, Tara Chelioudakis, Taz Bright, Seth McVey, Adam Smith, Connie Saylor, Caleb Peavy, Jessica Smith, Alex Zenk, Nick Campbell, Katie, Leanne, Hasti, and many others. I love my Christian family!

Thank you to Nicole Neville for your much-needed and appreciated daily help with the 2018 One Year Bible Support Group. Thank you also for your support as we contacted my foreign publishers and asked them to stop printing and selling my old heretical products.

Thank you for my continuing discernment education from Justin Peters, Paul Washer, Costi Hinn, Ray Comfort, Brandon Kimber, Holly Pivec, Marcia Montenegro, Michelle Lesley, Amy Spreeman, Todd Miles, Josh Mathews, J. Carl Laney, John MacArthur, Brad Bigney, Jeremiah Roberts, Andrew Soncrant, Mike Moore, and everyone in the NAR Heresy and Thy Word Is Truth groups. Thank you to my seminary professors and administrators: *I've learned so much from you!*

Thank you to my pastors and church family. I never imagined that I'd be part of a Christian fellowship community, and you have so warmly accepted Michael and me in ways that have healed our hearts. Your biblically solid sermons and our times of worship together are heavenly and deeply appreciated.

Thank you to everyone who prayed for my salvation during my years cloaked in New Age darkness, including Faith and Justice Collier. I'm so grateful that you cared enough to pray for my soul through those years. I also appreciate the encouraging letters of support I've received from people following my conversion. Each letter means a lot to me. Thank you.

Thank you to Timothy Paulson, Joel Kneedler, Kristen Golden,

Janene MacIvor, Darcie C. Robertson, and everyone at Thomas Nelson Publishers for answering my prayers that God would use my past to glorify Him. It is a joy to work with you all!

Thank you to those who have read my books, watched my videos, and attended my workshops during my New Age years and who've stayed with me as I proclaim my love for Jesus and share the gospel. I apologize for the messiness of my conversion, and for any confusion or hurt feelings you may have experienced as I first struggled to understand this big change, and as I continue to discuss the deception of New Age teachings and practices.

I also *deeply* apologize to those who were hurt or offended by the work I previously did in the New Age, or who were hurt or offended by my conversion to Christianity. I am truly sorry, and I pray that you will someday understand that I was deceived at the time, and that you will forgive me.

I have repented to God for my previous heretical teachings in the New Age, and I humbly apologize to the church body that my New Age work helped to popularize mystical experiences over sound biblical teachings. I pray that this book raises awareness of the undercover way that Satan is using New Age teachings to obscure the gospel message and to lead people astray.

Love,
Doreen

APPENDIX 1

10 Reasons Why New Age and Christianity Cannot Blend

I tried to blend New Age and Christianity for many years. Here are just ten of the many reasons why Christianity and the New Age are opposites that can never be blended:

1. New Age glorifies the self; Christianity glorifies God.
2. New Age says, "Follow your heart and do whatever makes you happy." Christianity says, "Follow and obey Jesus, for the heart is deceitful."
3. New Age turns to ascended masters, spirit guides, the universe, astrology, and angels for help; Christianity only follows the Holy Trinity.
4. New Age tries to predict and control the future; Christianity trusts God with the future.
5. New Age says there is no sin, hell, devil, or demons; Christianity believes Jesus' teachings about sin, hell, the devil, and demons in the Holy Bible.

6. New Age relies on channeled books, cards, and psychic readings for guidance; Christianity relies on prayer and the Bible.

7. New Age says Jesus is an "ascended master" or "just a man who was enlightened," and they imagine that Jesus is an "anything goes," laid-back man; Christianity says that Jesus was fully God and fully man during His earthly ministry, and He's now at the right hand of our heavenly Father God as the second member of the Holy Trinity. We will all stand before God on Judgment Day, and we want Jesus there with us to attest that we've been forgiven for our sins.

8. New Age says you get into heaven by "being a good person"; Christianity says it's not your works that save you—it's God's grace through your faith in the life, death, and resurrection of our Savior Jesus (who was the only sinless and truly good person to walk the earth). God's love doesn't give us license to do whatever we please.

9. New Age tries to "manifest" their wants and desires; Christianity trusts God's promise to meet the needs of believers.

10. New Age says there are many paths to God; Christianity quotes Jesus' own words: "I am the way, and the truth, and the life. No one comes to the Father except through me" (John 14:6).

APPENDIX 2

New Age Lingo

Some people don't realize they're becoming ensnared in New Age teachings, because it can happen gradually. The temptations that the New Age offers—happiness, peace, and success—are identical to what the serpent offered Eve in the garden and Jesus in the wilderness. Don't fall for his lies.

Beware of any person, song, movie, book, program, T-shirt, and so forth that uses these terms, as they're a signal of heretical and unbiblical teachings. I know these terms well because I regrettably used and taught them myself when I was under the spell of New Age deception:

abundance: a term used in the New Age to describe attracting and manifesting money, cars, homes, and other provisions. Your thoughts, energy, vision board, affirmations, and/or karma are seen to be the "source" of your supply, instead of acknowledging our sovereign God as the supplier of all that is good (Matthew 6:25–34; Philippians 4:19).

activation: the belief that you or a teacher can start or initiate some special healing gift. The Bible clearly says that only the Holy Spirit can activate and impart spiritual gifts according to His will (1 Corinthians 12:7–11). New Agers speak about "spiritual gifts" in unbiblical ways, such as saying they have the gift of ascension, DNA healing, violet flame activation, and so forth.

Akashic records: a New Age version of the Lamb's Book of Life (Philippians 4:3; Revelation 3:5, 13:8, 17:8, 20:15, 21:27), where the names and records of people are kept in determination of their eternal destiny.

alchemist: one who practices alchemy. See next.

alchemy: Originally, the word *alchemy* was defined as the medieval science or theory that endeavored to convert regular metals into precious metals. People tried all sorts of physical and mental-power formulas. Today, New Agers use this term as a synonym for attracting, creating, or manifesting your wishes into reality.

all one: referring to pantheism, the belief that God is within everyone and everything.

archangels: the highest order of angels. New Agers believe in archangels acting as personal guardian angels, and their list of archangels includes names not found in the Bible.

asanas: Yoga poses that were originally designed as bowing down to Hindu deities.

ascended masters: religious and spiritual leaders, some mythical, who have "ascended" and are now helping humanity from the spirit world. New Agers believe that Jesus is an ascended master who works with deities such as Buddha.

ascension: refers to a person ascending rather than dying; eliminates their belief in repentance and judgment.

astral travel / astral projection: See "out-of-body experience."

astrology: The belief that you can know someone's personality or future by looking at the position of stars and planets at the time and place of a person's birth. The Bible strictly forbids the use of astrology and horoscopes (Deuteronomy 18:10–14; Isaiah 47:13–14). Although the Magi who visited baby Jesus may or may not have been astrologers, the Bible described but does not condone astrology. After all, Magi means "magician," and the Bible condemns magic as well. In addition, we see that the royal astrologers had limited abilities compared to God's prophet Daniel (Daniel 1:20; 2:27).

attracting: a "law of attraction" term, crediting a person with attracting goodness into his or her life by his or her own power of positive thinking.

aura: the glow around a person, said to be different colors depending on the person's character and mood.

automatic writing: an occult process of sitting quietly and asking a spirit being to give you messages that you in turn write down. People use automatic writing to contact God, Jesus, saints, angels, and departed loved ones, but these messages always contradict Scripture because these are demons masquerading as Jesus, angels, and so on.

cards: Similar to playing cards, these cards in the New Age and the occult have pictures, words, or messages on them to tell the future, give someone "a reading," or get a message from the spirit world. Demons take advantage of those who use cards, to give them messages that lead them away from the true Jesus.

centering: calming one's mind and body and focusing on a meditation or teaching.

chakra: an Eastern mystical Sanskrit term for supposed wheels of energy inside our bodies that control our physical, emotional, and spiritual health.

channeling: receiving messages from an unknown spirit. Often the spirit will lie that he's God, Jesus, the Holy Spirit, or an angel to gain your trust. Whether you're receiving the messages yourself, or reading a book by someone who received these messages (even from a teacher or book labeled as Christian), always test the spirits and compare everything against Scripture.

chart: as in "Having my chart done," refers to an astrological chart.

Christ consciousness: New Agers who think Jesus is a universal energy believe that we can all share his mind. They believe that we are all "ascending" in our consciousness toward the pinnacle Christ consciousness. They disregard the gospel and believe it's symbolic.

clairvoyance: seeing a vision either in your mind's eye or with your physical eyes, usually referring to a future event.

cord cutting: releasing someone or something that you consider negative.

cocreating: the belief that God needs our help or permission to direct His will.

crystal children: a supposed new race of highly sensitive and gentle children with supernatural abilities who will bring peace to the world.

crystal points: fingerlike points of crystals used in necklaces and divination work that are said to connect you to universal energy.

contemplative prayer: a form of Eastern meditation that sounds Christian, involving a "centering prayer" and repetitive chanting of a word to supposedly receive guidance from God. This is a dangerous practice that is not supported by Scripture and could lead to receiving false guidance or following your imagination.[1]

A Course in Miracles: Also referred to as "The Course," this is an occult channeled book (actually, three books in one) that is supposedly from Jesus, explaining what He meant in the Bible. In reality, the book is a doctrine of demons, designed to lull unsuspecting people into following the false Jesus and heretical gospel, and lure them away from following the real Jesus of the Bible.

decree: New Age terms for believing that if you say the right formulaic words, your prayer will be answered, instead of realizing that God's will is sovereign over answered prayer. In the Bible, only God and kings decree legalities and commandments. The modern use of the term *decree* as a way to gain health or wealth is not biblical.

earth angel: What was once a retro song is now a New Age term to describe someone who had a past life in another spiritual dimension, such as previously being an angel, fairy, wizard, or something else supernatural.

energy: When a New Ager uses the term *energy*, he or she is describing a subjective personal experience with someone or something as being "positive energy" or "negative energy." New Agers will subjectively monitor themselves to find whether the item/person leaves them feeling safe and happy (which they will credit as the item/person having "positive energy") or whether they feel frightened, frustrated, or angry with the item/person (which will earn that item/person a label of being "negative energy").

entity / entity group: a term loosely applied to spiritual beings, ranging from angels to aliens to spirit guides. The popular New Age books from "Abraham-Hicks" are said to be messages from an entity group of spirits collectively called "Abraham."

fairies: nature spirits who control the weather and plant growth and interact with humans.

fear-based: a negative term applied to any person who disagrees with the New Ager. It's also a synonym for saying that a person or place is filled with "negative energy."

feng shui: an ancient Eastern mystic practice of rearranging furniture, downsizing the number of items you have, and hanging crystals and small octagonal mirrors to bring in "good energy."

goddess: This includes goddess worship and calling one's self or others a goddess.

grounding: the action of focusing on the here and now, and to become aware of your body and thoughts, as opposed to being spacy or daydreaming.

Great White Brotherhood: a New Age phrase for the pantheon of "ascended masters" working together as a team, usually believing this occurs at Mount Shasta, California.

higher plane of consciousness: the belief that you can get more accurate answers from the spirit world and practices such as meditating.

higher self: Thought to be the "true self" that is one with God or the universe, the "higher self" is your mind without your ego.

horoscope: a diagram showing planets and signs of the zodiac that astrologers use to foretell an individual's future. *See* astrology.

implant: the belief that aliens implant electronic chips in people to track and control them.

Indigos / Indigo Children: children and young adults who are believed to possess extrasensory abilities beyond other generations. Indigos are described as highly sensitive, blunt, and bold truth-tellers with strong opinions.

journey: usually a Shamanic form of visualization and trance induced by plant-based hallucinogenic drugs.

judging / judgmental: To a New Ager, if you disagree with their beliefs or lifestyle, you are judging them and are a judgmental person. They will twist Scripture about judging and incorrectly say that God and Jesus never judge anyone.

karma: an Eastern mystical belief in retribution and those who do good receiving good in return, and those who do evil receiving evil in return. Similar to the "law of attraction," karma usually refers to reincarnation, and that if you do good in this life you will be rewarded in the next life here on earth.

law of attraction / LOA: A term popularized by the New Age book and movie *The Secret,* this is the belief that people are entirely responsible for everything that happens in their life, based on their negative or positive thoughts.

lay line: the belief that there are strong energy current pipelines connecting "sacred sites" (geographical locations that are deemed to have extra spiritual significance). New Agers will talk about "Michael lay lines" and "Mary lay lines," referring to energy pipelines connected to the archangel Michael and Mother Mary.

light body: a person's etheric or energy double, with the exact same body except it is nonphysical and is composed of electricity-like energy. It's not the soul or spirit; it's a separate body each of us supposedly has, that consists of glowing energy. Supposedly, you can "activate" this light body.

life purpose: A high percentage of New Age teachings are focused on finding your life purpose, which usually means choosing an enjoyable career that helps others while also paying your bills.

little God: the belief that people are evolving into gods who control creations, health, and wealth in their own lives and the lives of others.

lower energy: a euphemism for demons or negativity.

manifest / manifesting / manifestation: In the New Age, these terms refer to attracting health and wealth through positive thoughts and "being a good person." Other manifesting techniques include visualization, vision casting, and vision boards.

meditate / meditation: The New Age and Eastern forms of meditation involve focusing on a word ("mantra"); emptying one's mind; noticing one's thoughts, feelings, and sensations; and asking one's "higher self" or a spirit for answers. New Agers often use a "guided meditation," which means that someone describes a relaxing scenario designed to help the person receive an answer from a "spirit." This is different from biblical meditation from the Hebrew word *hagah*, which means to "sigh" or "murmur Scripture aloud," which in biblical Hebrew means to repeat Scripture in one's mind (Joshua 1:8; Psalm 1:2).

mediumship: contacting spirits of the dead for messages. This is a practice that God clearly forbids in the Bible (Deuteronomy 18:10–12; 1 Samuel 28). The spirits are demons pretending to be deceased loved ones, and the demons gives the medium accurate information in order to fool living people into disobeying God.

Mercury retrograde: an astrological term for the planet Mercury's cycles, which are said to negatively affect human communication, contracts, and electronics because Mercury is associated with the pagan deity of messages and communications.

Merkabah / Metatron's cube: The New Age name for their story of the geometrical shape that transported Enoch (of Noah's lineage) as he ascended and became the archangel Metatron. This story is loosely based on the Jewish mystic Kabbalah and the apocryphal 1 Enoch. While Enoch's name is in the canonical Bible, there is no Merkabah or Metatron. New Agers claim that by wearing or meditating on a Merkabah symbol, they can gain favor and power.

metaphysics / metaphysical / metaphysician: *Meta* means "above," and *physics* refers to the physical domain. So, metaphysics is "above the physical," or in

other words, "the spiritual." Metaphysics is the study of how to attract, create, or manifest your wishes into reality. It's an attempt to be your own god.

mind-body-spirit / MBS: New Age festivals, conferences, healing work, or
holistic therapy. This refers to the "whole person" as consisting of equal
parts mind, body, and spirit.

moon cycles: While the Bible discusses the new moon, and some holy days
are movable feasts depending on the moon cycles, this term means something entirely different to a New Ager. Moon cycles can mean a men-
strual period, or it can refer to the practice of ceremonies and the practice of acknowledging the moon's effect on one's life. For example, New
Agers believe they will receive a windfall during a new moon, and that
they should release the old during a full moon. New Agers also pay close
attention to the "type" of full moon, e.g., a blood moon, supermoon,
and so on. In addition, New Agers hold the astrological time of the full
and new moon as being significant, such as saying "full moon in Leo."

namaste: an ancient Sanskrit (Eastern language) term for recognizing "the
god within" yourself and others. This is obviously unbiblical and blasphemous, yet this term is used regularly in New Age and yoga circles.

NDE / near-death experience: New Agers pay more attention to people who
report having NDEs than they do to what the Bible says about heaven
and the afterlife. NDEs usually involve a person experiencing a form
of death and traveling out-of-body toward a bright light, where they
may be met by deceased loved ones and see religious figures as well as
beautiful environments, while reporting that they're bathed in euphoric
feelings. YouTube is also filled with NDE videos of people reporting
they visited hell, but this doesn't get as much attention in the New Age
because the word *hell* is considered a metaphor for life struggles and is
also deemed a negative topic to be avoided.

negative energy: a term to describe any person, item, thought, action,
or situation that elicits a reaction of fear, frustration, or anger. So, a
Christian may be accused of having "negative energy" as he or she discusses biblical concepts of repentance, sin, and hell with a New Ager.

OBE / out-of-body experience / soul travel / astral projection / astral travel:
the New Age practice of willing your conscious awareness to detach from
your physical experience. For example, the person's body is lying in bed,
while the person is consciously aware of spiritually "traveling" to another
dimension or a different physical location.

one spirit: the belief that God only created one spirit, of which we are all part
and to which we all belong. In this belief system, we are all connected
as one united being, and it's an illusion that we seem to be in separated
bodies that are separated from God.

past life: the belief that we live multiple lifetimes and reincarnate into a new
person each life. The Bible says that we die once and then comes judgment (Hebrews 9:27). Some conspiracy theorists argue that the Bible
originally spoke of reincarnation, which was later removed. There is no
record of this in the earliest Bible manuscripts and fragments, which
date to AD 150–250, well before Constantine, who conspiracy theorists
say supposedly removed references to reincarnation in the Bible at the
Council of Nicaea in AD 325.

pendulum: a divination tool, consisting of a crystal point on a chain that
one holds and watches as the crystal swings in a direction designated as
a "no" or "false" answer versus swinging toward a "yes" or "true" answer.
The Bible condemns divination in Deuteronomy 18:10–12.

positive affirmations: saying your desires as if they have already happened,
usually beginning the statement with the words, "I am." The New Age
belief is that our thoughts, and not God, create our reality.

positive energy / positivity: how New Agers describe a person, item, situation, thought, or experience that elicits or is associated with sensations
of euphoria, hope, security, and love. New Agers will trust these feelings
more than they'll trust the Bible or a person in authority.

power animal / spirit animal / familiar spirit / daemon: the spirit of a wild
animal or bird that New Agers believe hover around us to protect and
guide us. This isn't a deceased pet—this is a spiritual essence of a wolf,
leopard, eagle, and so on, that functions like a guardian angel.

power places: certain geographical areas that are believed to be centers of great spiritual power that you can receive by visiting those locations, such as Sedona, Arizona; Machu Picchu, Peru; and Glastonbury, England. (*See also* "vortex.")

prana / chi / life force energy: terms used to describe the energy and space of the universe that we supposedly can tap into through various breathing, healing, dietary, and yogic techniques.

prayers of protection: a New Age term for saying unbiblical prayers to spirit guides, the universe, angels, shields of light, or deceased people before engaging in unbiblical activities, with the hope that you'll be protected from negativity or harm while engaging in these activities. God does not provide protection to help people disobey Him and participate in sorcery, divination, witchcraft, or other sinful behaviors.

psychic surgery: the belief that a "psychic surgeon" can use his mind power to extract physical illness and intrusions from someone's physical body. In some practices, the psychic surgeon will use unsterilized knives to cut open the body, and knives or his fingers to reach into a person's nostrils, supposedly to extract disease-causing items.

quantum / quantum physics: New Agers frequently use the terms *quantum* and *quantum physics* to add credibility to their beliefs, even though they aren't quantum physicists.

reading: a divination session involving cards, crystals, psychics, and such, for the purpose of trying to see into the past or future in order to gain answers and messages. The Bible strictly and clearly forbids this practice (Deuteronomy 18:10–12).

regression: a past life regression session, consisting of hypnosis and guided meditation, to try to "remember" your past life. (*See also* "past life.")

Reiki: Supposedly, Reiki is a healing energy that we can channel through symbols and our hands to heal others. To become a Reiki healer, you need to be "attuned" by a Reiki master (for a substantial fee) in order to learn and use the symbols. Christians should be wary of the true source of Reiki.

reincarnation: (*See* "past life.")

release: getting rid of something negative or unwanted, usually beginning with "mentally releasing" what is unwanted, then trusting that the physical release will follow automatically.

remote viewing: the belief that you can see what other people are doing, or clearly see inside their homes, without needing to be physically present. Through "mind power," a New Age person believes that they can remotely view whomever and whatever they desire.

sacred geometry: geometric shapes that are supposed to lend energy or power to whomever wears or looks at the shapes.

sage / saging: Sage is a desert brush plant with wide leaves that are bundled and burned in their dried form similar to incense. Saging is borrowed from Native American spirituality, with the belief that waving around a "sage wand" (tied bundle of dried sage leaves) can cause negativity or evil spirits to leave.

Sananda: The New Age name for Jesus. They also call him "Yeshua," which is technically His true Hebrew name; however, the *reason* why they call Jesus "Yeshua" is because of an aversion to Christian terminology and Christianity.

sending you love and light / love and light: a New Age term of endearment to signify that the New Ager cares about you and your situation. It's the equivalent of a Christian saying, "I will pray for you."

shield: visualizing a bubble of protective light around yourself, your car, your home, and so on.

silver cord / astral cord: a term describing a spiritual umbilical cord attaching a person's soul to their physical body. New Agers say when they experience out-of-body travel, the silver cord keeps them from floating away, similar to an astronaut attached to their space capsule.

soul mate: that one special romantic partner that the New Ager believes is just for you. New Agers conduct different activities to try to "energetically attract" or "manifest" their soul mate. When they meet someone they believe is their soul mate, they marry or move in together quickly. The unrealistic expectation is that your soul mate will see eye to eye with you on everything and the relationship will be fairy-tale harmonious. When normal relationship problems arise, New Agers decide that this person wasn't their soul mate after all, and they leave or divorce the person. The cycle of searching for their soul mate continues. This is one reason why New Agers have multiple marriages or marriage-like relationships.

soul tie: Similar to soul mates in a nonromantic relationship, this is the belief that some people were hatched in a soul cluster before their incarnation into earthly bodies. When you meet a person from your soul cluster, you have a "soul tie" to that person and there's an instant recognition or familiarity.

soul travel: the belief that you can travel in your imagination to other physical places or other dimensions.

source or source energy: a New Age euphemism for "God," because the New Ager doesn't want to say God for various reasons (painful experiences at church, unanswered prayer resulting in lost faith because of unrealistic expectations about prayer, fears of offending others, a desire to look cool, and so on).

speak into existence: the New Age belief that we can create, attract, or manifest with the words that we choose. Some New Agers believe they can persuade or manipulate God to grant their wishes if they choose the right words. This belief denies the sovereignty of God and God's will. Prayer does work; however, it's on God's terms and not ours.

Spirit: A euphemism that some New Agers use to avoid terms they consider "too Christian," like God, Jesus, or angels. However, when you hear or read that a person is getting messages from "Spirit," this means they are allowing themselves to be a conduit for unknown and untrustworthy beings, probably demons.

spirit guide: someone other than God who is guiding you. A spirit guide is thought to be a deceased relative, an angel, or an interdimensional being.

star seed: the belief that we all originated from stardust, instead of the Genesis story of creation.

TM / Transcendental Meditation: Meditating upon a "mantra," which is a word given to you to think repeatedly about. Former TM teacher Joe Kellett, author of *Falling Down the TM Rabbit Hole*, says that TM can lead to chronic dissociation and spaceyness. Researchers Drs. Farias and Catherine Wikholm report negative consequences from TM.[2] Opening your mind up to a mantra can open a doorway for demonic oppression. Remember that the biblical definition of meditation (*hagah* in Hebrew) means to study Scripture.

Tantra: Tantra courses or sessions usually involve teachings about sexuality from a Hindu perspective.

The Course: (See *A Course in Miracles.*)

true self: the "higher self." (*See* "higher self.")

twin flame: Similar to the belief in a "soul mate," a twin flame is said to be your once-in-many-lifetimes mate. A soul mate is your ideal mate in this life, while the New Age belief in reincarnation holds that a twin flame is your ideal mate from a past life who would also be your ideal mate in this life. Twin flame relationships are held out to be the pinnacle and are viewed as being as rare as a unicorn in a city zoo. New Agers will tell you that their twin flame didn't incarnate in this lifetime, but he or she is their spirit guide instead of their physical lover.

universe, the: To the New Ager, the universe is a synonym for God. Some New Agers believe that God is the universe, and other New Agers are shy about saying the name of God because they associate His name with painful experiences at church or unanswered prayer, or because they fear that saying the name of God will offend others. New Agers frequently "pray" to the universe for favor.

vibes: the feelings you experience when you're with someone or after visiting a certain place (e.g., "I got good vibes from that person," or "That place was filled with bad vibes"). New Agers also consciously try to send out "good vibes" so they can attract or create a specific wish into reality.

vision board: magazine pictures representing your wishes, pasted onto construction paper. You're supposed to stare at these pictures and imagine that's you, with the thin body, new car, and wonderful spouse, enjoying your vacation together. This process can temporarily work; however, the results are unsatisfying and don't last.

vision casting / casting a vision: Like a spiritual fisherman throwing a net or hook into the sea, this New Age belief is that you can attract, create, or manifest your wishes into reality if you imagine yourself "throwing" the visions out into "the ethers" or "the universe" or "to God," with the hope that you'll catch yourself a big fish equivalent of your wishes becoming reality.

visualize / visualization: the New Age practice of trying to get something in return by holding a vision of what you want. Sometimes this practice actually works; however, the results are temporary, unsatisfying, and differ from a person's expectations that happiness and lasting peace will be the end result.

vortex: the New Age belief that there are swirling energy vortexes beneath certain "power places" or "sacred spots" in the earth, such as Sedona, Arizona, or Glastonbury, England—both places that have a high number of New Age shops and healing centers. New Agers will lie down on the ground where these "vortexes" have been mapped, to absorb the power of the energy. (*See also* "power places.")

walking the labyrinth: A labyrinth is a path that usually leads inward in a circular design, which has been used for prayer and contemplation by many cultures since ancient times. New Agers use labyrinths for Eastern forms of meditation, goddess worship, and other unbiblical practices. The Bible warns us against ritualized forms of prayer (Matthew 6:5–8), so Christians should use extreme caution and biblical discernment with labyrinths.

yoga: the Hindu practice of bowing to pagan deities through poses called "asanas," a practice made popular in the West by New Agers. Even if a Christian were to use Scripture or hymns, each of these postures is still designed to worship pagan deities. Many yoga studios are filled with pagan statues and the use of blasphemous Sanskrit chanting.

your tribe / my tribe: terms that New Agers use for their group of like-minded friends.

Recommended Resources

Documentaries and Videos
(all available on YouTube)

American Gospel: Christ Alone
Charles Spurgeon: The People's Preacher
Clouds Without Water: Justin Peters
Crazy Bible: Ray Comfort
Evolution vs. God: Ray Comfort
Hell's Best Kept Secret: Ray Comfort and Kirk Cameron
Patterns of Evidence: Exodus
Paul Washer's "Shocking Youth Message"
Strange Fire Conference: John MacArthur and others
The Fool: Ray Comfort
Unpopular: The Movie

Books

Angels by Michael Heiser
A God of Many Understandings by Todd Miles

RECOMMENDED RESOURCES

Banana Man by Ray Comfort

Defining Deception by Costi W. Hinn and Anthony G. Wood

God, Greed, and the (Prosperity) Gospel by Costi W. Hinn

Gospel Treason by Brad Bigney

Hell's Best Kept Secret by Ray Comfort

Kingdom of the Cults by Walter Martin

Morning by Morning by Charles Spurgeon and Alistair Begg

My Utmost for His Highest by Oswald Chambers

Narrow Gate, Narrow Way by Paul Washer

Reformation Study Bible by R. C. Sproul

Richard Rohr and the Enneagram Secret, by Don and Joy Veinot
    and Marcia Montenegro

The Second Coming of the New Age by Steven Bancarz and Josh Peck

The Holiness of God by R. C. Sproul

The Holy Bible: ESV, KJV, NKJV, NIV, NLT, or NASB translations

The Light That Was Dark by Warren B. Smith

The Narrow Path by Tara Cherlioudakis

The Strategy of Satan by Warren Wiersbe

The Word-Faith Controversy by Robert Bowman

Truth or Territory by Jim Osman and Justin Peters

Radio Stations

Christian Satellite Network (CSN International)

RefNet Christian Radio

Websites with Helpful Blogs
About Avoiding Deception

AlisaChilders.com

BereanResearch.org

RECOMMENDED RESOURCES

CARM.org (Christian Apologetics & Research Ministry)
ChristianAnswersForTheNewAge.org
ChristIsTheCure.org
CSNTM.org (The Center for the Study of New Testament Manuscripts)
DanielBWallace.com
DrMSH.com (Dr. Michael Heiser)
EnduringWord.com
ForTheGospel.org
GotQuestions.org
HopeForLifeOnline.com
JustinPeters.org
Ligonier.org
LivingWaters.com
MichelleLesley.com
MidwestOutreach.org
PatternsOfEvidence.com
PirateChristian.com
ReasonsForJesus.com
SpiritOfError.org
TheCultishShow.com
TheMessedUpChurch.com
NewAgeToAmazingGrace.com
WesleyHuff.com
WeWouldRatherHaveJesus.com
Wretched.org

YouTube Channels

The Beat by Allen Parr
Allie Beth Stuckey

RECOMMENDED RESOURCES

Brother Matthew
Dale Partridge
David Guzik
Fighting for the Faith
FringePop321
G3 Conference
Got Questions Ministries
Justin Peters Ministries
Ligonier Ministries
Lindsay Davis
Melissa Dougherty
Michelle Lesley
Redeemer Bible Church
Steven Bancarz
Steven Kozar
Warren B. Smith
Wretched TV

Bibliography

Baker, M. D. *The Emerging Church, The Church, and You*. Fresno, CA: Hope for Life Online, 2019.

Bakon, Shimon. "True and False Prophets." *Jewish Bible Quarterly* 39, no. 3 (July–Sept. 2011): 152–58.

Bancarz, S., and J. Peck. *The Second Coming of the New Age*. Crane, MO: Defender Publishing, 2018.

Beale, G. K. *We Become What We Worship: A Biblical Theology of Idolatry*. Downers Grove, IL: InterVarsity Press, 2008.

Begg, Alistair. "Itching Ears." *Guard the Truth* 4, 2 Timothy 4:3–4 (January 2015): https://www.truthforlife.org/resources/sermon/itching-ears/.

Bickel, B., and S. Jantz. *World Religions & Cults 101*. Eugene, OR: Harvest House, 2002.

Bigney, B. *Gospel Treason: Betraying the Gospel with Hidden Idols*. Phillipsburg, NJ: P&R, 2012.

Bowman, R. M. *The Word-Faith Controversy*. Grand Rapids, MI: Baker Books, 2001.

Byron, John. "Paul and the Python Girl (Acts 16:16–19)." *Ashland Theological Journal* 41 (2009): 5–10.

Carson, D. A., R. T. France, J. Alec Motyer, and Gordon J. Wenham, eds. *New Bible Commentary*. Downers Grove, IL: IVP Academic Press, 1994.

Comfort, Ray. *Banana Man: The True Story of How a Demeaning Nickname Opened Amazing Doors for the Gospel*. Newberry, FL: Bridge-Logos, 2017.

———. "Ray Comfort's new movie, 'The Fool' helps those who've been bullied for their faith." YouTube. Doreen Virtue (August 27, 2018): https://www.youtube.com/watch?v=n_uBZFIJpGQ.

Derrett, J. D. "Simon Magus (Acts 8:9–24)." *Zeitschrift für die neutestamentliche Wissenschaft und die Kunde der älteren Kirche* 73, no 1–2 (1982): 52–68.

Doyle, T., and G. Webster. *Dreams and Visions: Is God Awakening the Muslim World?* Nashville: Thomas Nelson, 2012.

Duguid, I. A. *The Whole Armor of God: How Christ's Victory Strengthens Us for Spiritual Warfare*. Wheaton, IL: 2019.

ESV Study Bible, Wheaton, IL: Crossway, 2001.

Frame, J. M. *The Doctrine of the Christian Life*. Phillipsburg, NJ: P&R, 2008.

Geivett, R. D., and H. Pivec. *God's Super-Apostles*. Bellingham, WA: Lexham Press, 2014.

Got Questions Ministries. "Can Demons Attach Themselves to Non-Living/Inanimate Objects?" https://www.gotquestions.org/demons-objects.html.

———. "Who Was Simon the Sorcerer?" https://www.gotquestions.org/Simon-the-Sorcerer.html.

Guzik, D. *Verse by Verse Commentary on the Book of Exodus*. Santa Barbara, CA: Enduring Word Media, 2015.

Hawthorne, G. F. *Dictionary of Paul and His Letters*. Downers Grove, IL: InterVarsity Press, 1993.

Heiser, M. S. *Angels: What the Bible Really Says About God's Heavenly Host*. Bellingham, WA: Lexham Press, 2018.

Jacobson, R. A. "Moses, the Golden Calf, and the False Images of the True God." *Word & World Journal* 33, no. 2 (Spring 2013): 130–39.

Kent, G. J. R. "'Call up Samuel': Who Appeared to the Witch at En-Dor? (1 Samuel 28:3–25)." *Andrews University Seminary Studies* 52, no. 2 (Autumn 2014): 141–60.

Laney, J. Carl. *Essential Bible Background.* CreateSpace, 2016.

Leslie, S. H. *Dominionism and the Rise of Christian Imperialism.* Ravenna, OH: Conscience Press, 2005.

Lewis, C. S. *The Screwtape Letters.* San Francisco: HarperOne, 2015.

Lloyd-Jones, D. M. *Fellowship with God,* Wheaton, IL: Crossway, 2012, 6–19.

———. *Studies in the Sermon on the Mount.* Grand Rapids: Eerdmans, 1984, 63.

Lunn, N. P. "Patterns in the Old Testament Metanarrative: Human Attempts to Fulfill Divine Promises." *Westminster Theological Journal* 72, no. 2 (Fall 2010): 237–49.

Mackie, T. *Esther: Literary Design & Main Themes.* Portland, OR: Western Seminary.

Martin, W. *The Kingdom of the Cults.* Minneapolis, MN: Bethany House, 2019.

McConnell, D. R. "The Kenyon Connection: A Theological and Historical Analysis of the Cultic Origins of the Faith Movement." Quoted in Robert M. Bowman Jr. *The Word-Faith Controversy.* Grand Rapids, MI: Baker, 2001.

Miles, T. L. *A God of Many Understandings? The Gospel and a Theology of Religions.* Nashville, TN: B&H Publishing Group, 2010.

Miller, P. D. "The Story of the First Commandment: The Book of Exodus." *American Baptist Quarterly* 21, no. 2 (June 2002): 234–46.

Milmine, G. *The Life of Mary Baker Eddy and the History of Christian Science* (1909). University of Nebraska Press, 1993.

Montenegro, Marcia. "Enneagram Hidden Truth." YouTube. Doreen Virtue (October 2, 2019): https://www.youtube.com/watch?v=cipmC_pFyys.

Motyer, J. A. "Idolatry." *The Illustrated Bible Dictionary.* Edited by J. D. Douglas. Leicester, UK: InterVarsity Press, 1980, 2:680.

Mounce, W. D. *Mounce's Complete Expository Dictionary of Old & New Testament Words.* Grand Rapids, MI: Zondervan, 2006.

New Dictionary of Biblical Theology. Downers Grove, IL: InterVarsity Press, 2000.

NKJV Cultural Backgrounds Study Bible. Grand Rapids, MI: Zondervan, 2017.

One Year Bible. New Living Translation. Carol Stream, IL: Tyndale House, 2004.

Osman, J. *Truth or Territory: A Biblical Approach to Spiritual Warfare.* Kootenai, ID: Kootenai Community Church Publishing, 2015.

Parsons, B. "How Can I Avoid Becoming Prideful?" Ligonier-Ministries, 2019.

Peters, J. "Spiritual Healing: Justin Peters Conversation." YouTube. Doreen Virtue (November 25, 2019): https://www.youtube.com/watch?v=1ZWWNljQDxw.

Pink, A. W. *Gleanings in Exodus.* Chicago: Moody Press, 1981.

Quash, B., and M. Ward. *Heresies and How to Avoid Them: Why It Matters What Christians Believe.* Grand Rapids, MI: Baker Academic, 2007.

Reeves, K. *D is for Deception: The Language of the "New" Christianity.* Eureka, MT: Lighthouse Trails, 2016.

Robertson, Edward. "'Ūrīm and Tummīm: What Were They?" *Vetus Testamentum* 14, no. 1 (January 1964): 67–74.

Rosebrough, C. "Confessions of a Repentant False Prophet." YouTube. Fighting for the Faith (December 17, 2019): https://www.youtube.com/watch?v=q7-RHo7bHog.

Ryle, J. C. *Expository Thoughts on the Gospels: Matthew.* Grand Rapids, MI: Baker Book House, 2007.

———. *Flee from Idolatry.* Pensacola, FL: Chapel Library, 2004.

Sire, J. W. *Scripture Twisting: 20 Ways the Cults Misread the Bible.* Downers Grove, IL: IVP Books, 1980.

Smith, W. B. *False Christ Coming: What New Age Leaders Really Have in Store for America, the Church, and the World.* Magalia, CA: Mountain Stream Press, 2011.

———. *The Light That Was Dark: From the New Age to Amazing Grace.* Magalia, CA: Mountain Stream Press, 2005.

Smith, J. "Why I Stopped Teaching Yoga and Reiki, to Follow Jesus— Jessica Smith Interview." YouTube. Doreen Virtue (November 16, 2019): https://www.youtube.com/watch?v=AkiNFjzJ6y4.

Sproul, R. C. *The Holiness of God*. Wheaton, IL: Tyndale House, 1998.

———. *The Mystery of the Holy Spirit*. Wheaton, IL; Tyndale House, 1990.

———. *The Reformation Study Bible*. Orlando, FL: Ligonier Ministries, 2005.

———. *The Reformation Study Bible*. Sanford, FL: Reformation Trust, 2015.

———. *Truths We Confess*. Sanford, FL: Reformation Trust, 2019.

Spurgeon, C. H. *Spurgeon's Gems: Words of Wisdom from the Writings of C.H. Spurgeon*. Apollo, PA: Ichthus Publications, 2014.

———. *The Complete Works of C.H. Spurgeon 51, Sermons 2916 to 2967*. Fort Collins, CO: Delmarva Publications.

Vanhoozer, K. J. *Dictionary for Theological Interpretation of the Bible*. Grand Rapids, MI: Baker Academic, 2005.

Vine, W. E. *Vine's Complete Expository Dictionary with Topical Index*. Nashville: Thomas Nelson, 1996.

Washer, P. *Narrow Gate, Narrow Way*. Grand Rapids, MI: Reformation Heritage Books, 2018.

"Why We Should Avoid Bethel Music," YouTube. Doreen Virtue (November 20, 2019): https://www.youtube.com/watch?v=BYX3N50Pj7w.

Wiersbe, W. W. *The Bible Exposition Commentary*. Colorado Springs, CO: Cook Communications Ministries, 2001.

Wilson, M. K. "'As You Like It': The Idolatry of Micah and the Danites (Judges 17–18)." *ReformedTheological Review* 54, no. 2 (May–August 1995): 73–85.

Yungen, R. *Five Things You Should Know About Contemplative Prayer*. Eureka, MT: Lighthouse Trails, 2013.

Notes

Introduction

1. Charles H. Spurgeon, *The Complete Works of C. H. Spurgeon, vol. 12, Sermons 668 to 727* (Fort Collins, CO: Delmarva, 2013), 628.
2. Mary Baker Eddy, *Science and Health with Key to the Scriptures* (Boston: Christian Science , 1934), 25:6; 45:32–46:3; 330:25–27; 333:3–15; 447:24; 469:13–17; 470:9–14.
3. R. C. Sproul, *The Reformation Study Bible* (Orlando: Ligonier Ministries, 2005), 1540.
4. Ray Yungen, *Five Things You Should Know About Contemplative Prayer* (Eureka, MT: Lighthouse Trails, 2013), 9.
5. William Edwy Vine, *Vine's Complete Expository Dictionary with Topical Index* (Nashville: Thomas Nelson, 1996), 150.
6. Eddy, *Science and Health with Key to the Scriptures*, 586:1.
7. James W. Sire, *Scripture Twisting: 20 Ways the Cults Misread the Bible* (Downers Grove, IL: IVP Books, 1980), 92–93.
8. Sire, *Scripture Twisting*, 66–67.
9. Georgine Milmine, *The Life of Mary Baker Eddy and the History of Christian Science* (Lincoln: University of Nebraska Press, 1993), loc. 1888.

10. Kevin J. Vanhoozer, *Dictionary for Theological Interpretation of the Bible* (Grand Rapids: Baker Academic, 2005), 58.

Chapter 1: The Woman at the Well

1. Walter Martin, *The Kingdom of the Cults* (Minneapolis: Bethany House, 2019), 168–70.
2. Martin, *Kingdom of the Cults*, 169.
3. Robert M. Bowman Jr., *The Word-Faith Controversy* (Grand Rapids: Baker Books, 2001), 43–55.
4. Daniel R. McConnell, "The Kenyon Connection: A Theological and Historical Analysis of the Cultic Origins of the Faith Movement" (master's thesis, Oral Roberts University, 1982), 106, quoted in Bowman, *The Word-Faith Controversy*, 48.
5. Justin Peters, "Spiritual Healing: Justin Peters conversation," Doreen Virtue, November 25, 2019, YouTube video, 1:03:45, https://www.you tube.com/watch?v=1ZWWNljQDxw&t=1s.

Chapter 2: Testing the Spirits

1. R. C. Sproul, *The Holiness of God* (Wheaton, IL: Tyndale House, 1998), 37–38.
2. Kevin Reeves, *D is for Deception: The Language of the "New" Christianity* (Eureka, MT: Lighthouse Trails, 2016), 14.
3. Warren W. Wiersbe, *The Bible Exposition Commentary* (Colorado Springs: Cook Communications Ministries, 2001), 241.
4. "4 Reasons Spurgeon Died Poor," The Spurgeon Center, October 10, 2016, https://www.spurgeon.org/resource-library/blog-entries/4-reasons -spurgeon-died-poor.
5. J. C. Ryle, *Expository Thoughts on the Gospels: Matthew* (New York: Robert Carter & Brothers, 1860), 68–69.

Chapter 3: Sin Was a Four-Letter Word

1. Gerald F. Hawthorne, Ralph P. Martin, and Daniel G. Reid, eds., *Dictionary of Paul and His Letters* (Downers Grove, IL: InterVarsity Press, 1993), 352.

Chapter 4: Rock-Star Lifestyle

1. Costi Hinn, *God, Greed, and the (Prosperity) Gospel* (Grand Rapids: Zondervan, 2019), 57.
2. Hinn, *God, Greed, and the (Prosperity) Gospel*, 134.
3. Burk Parsons, "How Can I Avoid Becoming Prideful?" Ligonier Ministries, December 2, 2019, YouTube video, 2:48, https://www.youtube.com/watch?v=eMeCeq-sMLs.
4. T. Desmond Alexander et al., eds., *New Dictionary of Biblical Theology* (Downers Grove, IL: InterVarsity Press, 2000), 212.

Chapter 5: False Prophecy

1. Michael S. Heiser, *Angels: What the Bible Really Says About God's Heavenly Host* (Bellingham, WA: Lexham Press, 2018), 68–73.
2. Ancient Hindu documents teach the link between yoga and worshiping deities, including Patanjali's *Yoga-sutras* (400 BC), Shvetashvatara Upanishad and the *Bhagavad Gita*, especially in the sections concerning bhakti yoga, an ancient practice of joining with a personal deity. For a modern recap of these teachings, please see Colleen Morton Busch, "The Heroes, Saints, and Sages Behind Yoga Pose Names," Yoga Journal, updated April 5, 2017, https://www.yogajournal.com/yoga-101/heroes-saints-sages#comments.
3. R. C. Sproul, *Truths We Confess* (Sanford, FL: Reformation Trust, 2019), 135–37.
4. Bruce Bickel and Stan Jantz, *World Religions & Cults 101* (Eugene, OR: Harvest House, 2002), 136–38.

Chapter 6: Apostasy, Heresy, and Confusion

1. Ben Quash and Michael Ward, *Heresies and How to Avoid Them: Why It Matters What Christians Believe* (Grand Rapids: Baker Academic, 2007), 15, 24, 50.
2. Sarah H. Leslie, *Dominionism and the Rise of Christian Imperialism* (Ravenna, OH: Conscience Press, 2005).
3. Sproul, *Truths We Confess*, 202, (see chap. 5, n. 3).
4. Todd L. Miles, *A God of Many Understandings? The Gospel and a Theology of Religions* (Nashville: B&H, 2010), 16–18.
5. Miles, *A God of Many Understandings?*, 162–63.

6. Ray Comfort, *Banana Man: The True Story of How a Demeaning Nickname Opened Amazing Doors for the Gospel* (Newberry, FL: Bridge-Logos, 2017), 118–19.

7. Ray Comfort, "Are You a Good Person?" Living Waters, January 19, 2018, https://www.livingwaters.com/are-you-a-good-person/.

8. Ray Comfort, "Ray Comfort's New Movie, 'The Fool' Helps Those Who've Been Bullied for Their Faith," Doreen Virtue, August 27, 2018, YouTube video, 57:45, https://www.youtube.com/watch?v=n_uBZFIJpGQ&t=2s.

9. Miles, *A God of Many Understandings?*, 117.

10. Peters, "Spiritual Healing," (see chap. 1, n. 5).

Chapter 7: Worshiping the Creation Instead of the Creator

1. D. Martyn Lloyd-Jones, *Fellowship with God* (Wheaton, IL: Crossway, 2012), 16–19.

2. Warren B. Smith, *False Christ Coming: Does Anybody Care?: What New Age Leaders Really Have in Store for America, the Church, and the World* (Ashland, OH: Mountain Stream Press, 2011), 15–16.

3. D. Martyn Lloyd-Jones, *Studies in the Sermon on the Mount* (Grand Rapids: Eerdmans, 1984), p. 63.

4. Alistair Begg, "Itching Ears," Truth for Life, January 11, 2015, audio recording, 39:00, https://www.truthforlife.org/resources/sermon/itching-ears/.

5. Paul Washer, *Narrow Gate, Narrow Way* (Grand Rapids: Reformation Heritage Books, 2018), 24.

6. Shimon Bakon, "True and False Prophets," *Jewish Bible Quarterly* 39, no. 3 (July–September 2011): 152–58.

Chapter 8: The False Christ of the New Age

1. D. A. Carson et al., eds., *New Bible Commentary* (Downers Grove, IL: IVP Academic, 1994), 964–65.

Chapter 9: Church Shopping

1. Doreen Virtue, "Confessions of a Repentant False Prophet," Fighting for the Faith, December 18, 2019, YouTube video, 1:14:03, https://www.youtube.com/watch?v=q7-RHo7bHog&t=3s.

2. Tom Doyle with Greg Webster, *Dreams and Visions: Is Jesus Awakening the Muslim World?* (Nashville: Thomas Nelson, 2012).

3. Darren Carlson, "When Muslims Dream of Jesus," The Gospel Coalition, May 31, 2018, https://www.thegospelcoalition.org/article/muslims-dream-jesus/.

4. Edward Robertson, "The Ūrīm and Tummīm; What Were They?," *Vetus Testamentum* 14, no. 1 (January 1964): 67–74.

5. Warren B. Smith, *The Light That Was Dark* (Magalia, CA: Mountain Stream Press, 2005).

6. *The One Year Bible*, New Living Translation (Carol Stream, IL: Tyndale House, 2004).

Chapter 10: Tossing the Idols

1. "Can Demons Attach Themselves to Non-Living/Inanimate Objects?" Got Questions, https://www.gotquestions.org/demons-objects.html.

2. Steven Bancarz and Josh Peck, *The Second Coming of the New Age* (Crane, MO: Defender Publishing, 2018), 361.

3. William D. Mounce, ed., *Mounce's Complete Expository Dictionary of Old & New Testament Words* (Grand Rapids: Zondervan, 2006), 351.

4. J. A. Motyer, "Idolatry," in *Illustrated Bible Dictionary*, ed. J. D. Douglas (Leicester, UK: InterVarsity Press, 1980): 2:680.

5. Mounce, *Mounce's Complete Expository Dictionary*, 349–50.

6. Brad Bigney, *Gospel Treason: Betraying the Gospel with Hidden Idols* (Phillipsburg, NJ: P&R, 2012), 24–25.

7. G. K. Beale, *We Become What We Worship: A Biblical Theology of Idolatry* (Downers Grove, IL: InterVarsity Press, 2008), 127, 133.

Chapter 11: Sanctification in the Public Eye

1. Mark D. Baker, *The Emerging Church, the Church, and You* (Fresno: Hope for Life Online, 2019), 3–4.

2. Timothy Mackie, *Esther: Literary Design & Main Themes* (Portland: Western Seminary).

3. D. A. Carson et al., *New Dictionary of Biblical Theology* (Downers Grove: IL: InterVarsity Press, 2000), 198.

4. Mackie, *Esther*, xx.

Chapter 12: Repentance

1. Grenville J. R. Kent, " 'Call up Samuel': Who Appeared to the Witch at En-Dor? (1 Samuel 28:3–25)," *Andrews University Seminary Studies* 52, no. 2 (Autumn 2014): 141–60.

2. John Byron, "Paul and the Python Girl (Acts 16:16–19),"*Ashland Theological Journal* 41 (2009), 5–10.

3. J. Duncan M. Derrett, "Simon Magus (Acts 8:9–24)," *Zeitschrift für die neutestamentliche Wissenschaft und die Kunde der älteren Kirche* 73, no. 1–2 (1982), 52–68.

4. "Who Was Simon the Sorcerer?" Got Questions, https://www.got questions.org/Simon-the-Sorcerer.html.

5. R. Douglas Geivett and Holly Pivec, *God's Super-Apostles* (Bellingham, WA: Lexham Press, 2014), 70–78.

6. Geivett and Pivec, *God's Super-Apostles*, 71–72.

7. Kevin J. Vanhoozer, *Dictionary for Theological Interpretation of the Bible* (Grand Rapids: Baker Academics, 2005), 446.

Chapter 13: Spiritual Warfare

1. Jim Osman, *Truth or Territory: A Biblical Approach to Spiritual Warfare* (Kootenai, ID: Kootenai Community Church Publishing, 2015), 106–12.

2. John M. Frame, *The Doctrine of the Christian Life* (Phillipsburg, NJ: P&R, 2008), 255.

3. Iain M. Duguid, *The Whole Armor of God: How Christ's Victory Strengthens Us for Spiritual Warfare* (Wheaton, IL: Crossway, 2019), 25, 37, 51, 65, 77, 89.

4. C. S. Lewis, *The Screwtape Letters* (San Francisco: HarperOne, 2015).

5. Charles H. Spurgeon, *The Complete Works of C. H. Spurgeon, vol. 51, Sermons 2916 to 2967* (Fort Collins, CO: Delmarva, 2013), 221.

6. Charles H. Spurgeon, *Spurgeon's Gems: Words of Wisdom from the Writings of C. H. Spurgeon* (Apollo, PA: Ichthus, 2014), 174.

Chapter 14: Making New Friends

1. Steven Bancarz and Josh Peck, *The Second Coming of the New Age* (Crane, MO: Defender, 2018).

2. Judy Franklin and Ellyn Davis, *The Physics of Heaven* (Shippensburg, PA: Destiny Image, 2012), 49.

3. R. C. Sproul, *The Reformation Study Bible* (Sanford, FL: Reformation Trust, 2015), 1989.

4. "Why We Should Avoid Bethel Music," Doreen Virtue, November 20, 2019, YouTube video, 1:09:19, https://www.youtube.com/watch?v=BYX 3N50Pj7w&t=209s.

5. Jessica Smith, "Why I Stopped Teaching Yoga and Reiki, to Follow Jesus—Jessica Smith Interview," Doreen Virtue, November 16, 2019, YouTube video, 1:26:09, https://www.youtube.com/watch?v=AkiNFjz J6y4&t=1s.

6. Marcia Montenegro, "Enneagram Hidden Truth," Doreen Virtue, October 2, 2019, YouTube video, 1:07:01, https://youtu.be/cipmC_pFyys.

Appendix 2

1. Ray Yungen, *Five Things You Should Know About Contemplative Prayer* (Eureka, MT: Lighthouse Trails, 2013).

2. Dan Delzell, "Does Transcendental Meditation Trigger Depression and Psychosis?" *Christian Post*, June 9, 2015, https://www.christianpost .com/news/does-transcendental-meditation-trigger-depression-and -psychosis.html.

About the Author

Raised in Christian Science, Doreen Virtue was formerly the top-selling New Age author at the world's largest New Age publisher until Jesus opened her eyes to the gospel. She was baptized for the first time and began spreading the gospel message and denouncing the New Age. After being fired from her New Age publisher and losing most of her friends and some of her family members, enduring cruel slander and spiritual warfare, and losing her home, Doreen and her husband, Michael, began rebuilding their lives on the solid foundation of Jesus. They learned how to trust in God instead of trying to predict or control the future. Today they live in the Pacific Northwest where they attend a biblically solid church and Doreen attends seminary studying biblical theology so she won't be deceived again.

DoreenVirtue.com
Instagram.com/DoreenVirtue
Facebook.com/DoreenVirtueForJesus
YouTube.com/DoreenVirtueForJesus

9 780785 234104